Programming Languages and Compilers Quiz Book

A Compendium of ~1,400 short
questions, with answers

S.R. Subramanya

Exskillence

San Diego, USA

Table of Contents

Preface

The theory of programming languages is one of the fundamental courses in Computer Science. Programming languages have seen tremendous advancements over the years in terms of their features, expressive power, and convenience offered to programmer, and also in terms catering to the changing needs of applications (ex. Web-based applications) and security needs/aspects. Over the years several hundred different programming languages have been developed. Newer languages continue to be developed. Several of the languages developed decades ago continue to be used even today (through successive versions), and many others have faded away from mainstream use. However, there are only a handful of distinct programming language paradigms, namely, Procedural, Functional, Object-Oriented, Logic-programming, and Scripting languages. While some of the languages are purely interpretive languages, majority of the languages are compiled to machine code, and a few are compiled to an intermediate representation which is either interpreted or compiled to the final machine code. The Compiler techniques (program translation) have also seen phenomenal advancements. Modern compilers are routinely written in high-level languages. Also, the tools and techniques of compiler generators have seen tremendous advancements over the years.

A good understanding of the concepts underlying the theory of Programming Language would be very useful in the real-world of programming and software development. For students who are taking a course on Programming Languages or Compilers, or have already taken this course, or have otherwise learnt the topics of this course, there are not many comprehensive resources for a quick self-assessment of the fundamental understanding of the principles, concepts, and techniques of Programming Languages and Compilers. This book aims to fill that need. It has ~1,400 short questions with answers, covering all the major topics in a typical first course in Programming Languages. For details of the solution to any question, there are numerous textbooks and Web resources.

This is a quick assessment book / quiz book. It has a vast collection of a wide variety of questions on Programming Languages and Compilers. The book covers questions on the following topics: Overview of Programming Languages, Design and implementation of key aspects of some important/popular programming languages, Bindings and Scopes, Data types, Expressions and Assignment statements, Subprograms and

Parameter passing mechanisms, Abstract Data Types (in C++ and Java), Object-Oriented constructs (in C++ and Java), and Exception handling. The topics related to Compilers include programming language syntax and semantics, lexical analysis, parsing (syntax analysis), and different parsing techniques.

Unique features of this book

- ~ 1,400 short questions, with answers.
- Questions consist of True/False, sentence completion, and short essay-type questions.
- Questions have a wide range of difficulty levels.
- Many questions go beyond the straight-forward definitions.
- Questions are designed to test a deeper understanding of the topical material.
- Questions also cover questions possibly asked in internship / job interviews.

Who could benefit from this book?

- Students who are currently taking Programming Languages / Compilers course could use this book for self–assessment, and for improving performance in tests and exams.
- Students who have already finished a course on Programming Languages / Compilers, and are preparing to take written exams and/or interviews for industry/companies.
- Faculty can use it as a resource to quickly select a few questions as part of a quiz being prepared.
- Interviewers / Managers / Technical leads could use it to make a quick assessment of the candidates' fundamental understanding of concepts, in phone / personal interviews.

Notes

Only later version(s) of languages are considered with regard to their features.

Several of the features, unless otherwise specified, refer to those that are common to the C–family of languages.

C++ and Java have been elaborated during the discussion of certain features.

All abbreviations are expanded in their initial uses. They are also given below for convenience.

BNF – Backus-Naur Form
CFG – Context-Free Grammar
CFL – Context-Free Language
CLR Parser – Canonical LR Parser
DFA – Deterministic Finite Automaton
EBNF – Extended Backus-Naur Form
JSP – Java Server Pages
NFA – Non-deterministic Finite Automaton
PDA – Push-Down Automaton
LALR Parser – Look Ahead LR Parser
LL Parser – Left-to-Right, Left-most derivation parser
LR Parser – Left-to-right, Right-most derivation parser
RHS – Right Hand Side
SLR Parser – Simple LR Parser
XSLT – eXensible Stylesheet Language Transformations

Given below are a few programming languages with a brief outline of features, which were popular, or/and were influential in the design of other languages, or/and currently used in several application areas.

Ada – It is an imperative language with object-oriented features. It is strongly typed with the intent of minimizing inadvertent programming errors. It supports modular programs via packages. It has constructs for concurrent programming, message passing, and exception handling. Ada was originally designed for embedded and real-time systems.

ALGOL – It introduced the concept of code blocks, nested function definitions with lexical scope, and other features which led to the practice of structured programming. It has had much influence on the design of many programming languages, including CPL, Simula, BCPL, B, Pascal, C, etc.

APL – It is a programming language using multidimensional array as its central datatype. It enables writing very concise and powerful code by the use of several special symbols representing most functions and operators. It has had influence on the development of spreadsheets, functional programming, and computer math packages.

AWK – It was developed for use on UNIX systems text processing, data extraction, data formatting, and reporting. It is a scripting language. It makes extensive use of string datatype, associative arrays, and regular expressions.

BASIC – It was designed with primary aim of ease of use to enable non-specialists to be able to program. It was popular on 'home' and personal computers.

C – It is a general-purpose, procedural language. It provides bare essential features for developing very powerful programs. Several of the required functionalities not in the language is supported by several library routines. It has statements which can perform several assembly-level functions. It is widely used in programming embedded systems. It was the earliest of high-level languages used for systems programming (writing compilers, text editors, etc.). it has had considerable influence on C++, C#, Java, JavaScript Perl, PHP, Python,, Swift, Verilog, etc.

C++ – It is a language with C language as the basic of basic data types and control structures, and the addition of object-oriented features. It supports modularity via packages. It has support for exception handling. It is popular in systems programming, and widely used in programming embedded systems.

C# – It a procedural language with added object-oriented features. It has support for strong typing, array bounds checking, detection of uninitialized variables, and automatic garbage collection. It supports modularity via packages. It has support for exception handling. It also supports limited for functional programming through first-class functions.

COBOL – It is an imperative language with limited object-oriented features. It has some very high-level (almost English-like) constructs. It was the earliest of languages to introduce the notion of record type – a compound data type with heterogeneous members. It is primarily used in commercial data processing on mainframe computers, with large-scale batch and transaction processing jobs.

Eiffel – It is a pure object-oriented language, where the basic data types are based on classes. It supports multiple inheritance. It has garbage collection mechanism. It has concurrent programming constructs.

Fortran – It is an imperative language that is especially well suited to numeric computation and scientific computing. The recent versions have object-oriented features. It supports modularity. It has concurrent programming constructs.

Haskell – It is purely functional language, with functions (generally) having no side effects. It supports type safety and type-safe operator overloading.

Java – It is a class-based, object-oriented language with imperative control structures. It is highly portable language due to the fact that compilers generate an intermediate code (Java bytecode) that runs on any hardware, after interpretation/compilation on a particular machine. Java supports type checks. It has garbage collection mechanism, and support for exception handling. It is widely used in embedded systems and Web programming.

JavaScript – It is more of a scripting language with object-oriented features. It is dynamically typed, supports functions as first-class objects. It supports event-driven programming. JavaScript is widely used in web browsers.

Lisp – It is a functional language. It is the earliest language developed for Artificial Intelligence applications. List is the primary data structure in the language. It has garbage collection mechanism. It supports dynamic typing and functions as first-class objects.

ML – It is a functional language. ML. It supports type safety. ML has support for garbage collection. It is widely used in compiler writing, automated theorem proving, and formal verification.

Modula – It is an imperative language, with object-oriented features. It is a type-safe language and supports modular program development. It has support for garbage collection and exception handling. It has had influence on Java, C#, and Python.

Pascal – It is an imperative language. Pascal was an early language to support complex data types (ex. structs) and recursive data structures (ex. lists, trees). It is strongly typed. It supports nested subprogram definitions.

Perl – It is more of a scripting language which is mostly interpreted. It supports dynamic data typing and garbage collection. It supports automatic, dynamic type conversions.

PL/I – It is an imperative language. It is designed for scientific, engineering, business and system programming. It has English-like syntax. It supports modular program development and exception handling.

Prolog – It is a declarative, logic programming language. It is based on first-order logic. The program logic is expressed in terms of relations which consist of facts and rules. It is widely used in artificial intelligence, theorem proving, natural language processing, and computational linguistics applications.

Python – It is an imperative language with object-oriented features. It is dynamically typed and supports garbage collection. It supports dynamic binding (late binding), of method and variable names during program execution. It has support for use of functions as first-class objects. It supports modular program development and exception handling.

Scheme – It is a functional language. List is the central data structure used. It has support for functions as first-class objects. It has garbage collection.

Simula – It is considered the earliest of object-oriented languages. It supports classes, objects, inheritance, etc. It supports concurrent programming. It has support for garbage collection. It has had influence on many of the features of object-oriented languages including C++, Object Pascal, Java, C#, etc.

Smalltalk – It is a pure object-oriented language. The programs are usually compiled to bytecode, which is then interpreted by a virtual machine or translated into machine code. Computation primarily proceeds with messages sent to objects (unlike traditional control structures of imperative programming).

SNOBOL – It is a string-processing language. It has a rich set of operators for pattern matching and string manipulation. A pattern handled by SNOBOL can be even as complex as the complete grammar of a computer language. It has supports integers, real numbers, strings, patterns, arrays, and associative arrays as built-in data types. It supports user-defined data types and functions.

Questions

A. Preliminaries and Overview

True/False Questions

A1 In the early years of high–level language programming readability was not an important issue. _____

A2 Readability is not important in modern languages. _____

A3 Increasing writability/flexibility of a language (generally) leads to reduced reliability, and vice versa. _____

A4 Strict controls in a language to increase reliability leads to (relatively) higher cost of execution. _____

A5 Code from another file cannot be included in another file without explicitly copying it. _____

A6 The most prevalent category of programming languages is the nonprocedural languages. _____

A7 An object file contains the symbol table of the identifiers that are externally visible. _____

A8 The imperative languages are highly influenced by the von Neumann architecture. _____

A9 The assignment statement is not required in pure functional languages. _____

A10 There are no languages without reserved words. _____

A11 The reference to a function in a file, which has been defined in a different file, can be resolved at compile time. _____

A12 Dynamically typed languages are never strongly typed. _____

A13 A computer without the appropriate floating-point hardware can still perform floating-point operations using floating-point instructions emulator. _____

A14 Scripting languages are usually interpreted languages. _____

A15 Many contemporary languages do not allow nested subprograms. _____

A16 Pattern matching using regular expressions is not supported in any language. _____

A17 Inlining a function or method makes it more efficient. _____

A18 Inlined function or method eliminates the cost of linkage. _____

A19 The macros in a program are expanded during the compilation process. _____

A20 Translating a high-level language program to intermediate code helps portability. _____

A21 There is no guarantee that an arbitrary real numbers (floating-point) will have the exact values inside the computer. _____

A22 A floating-point variable can store the exact value within the allowable range of representation. _____

A23 The range of integer values is much less than those of real numbers (floating point, double precision) in computer representation. _____

A24 The result of compiling a program is always directly executable by the machine. _____

A25 An integer variable can store the exact value within the allowable range of representation. _____

A26 Interpreters are less portable than compilers. _____

A27 Code optimization is mandatory step in all compilers. _____

A28 Interpreters are slower than compilers. _____

A29 Interpreters do not require symbol table during interpretation. _____

A30 Hybrid implementation systems are slower than pure interpreters. _____

A31 Just-in-time (JIT) compilation translates the source code to the (executable) machine code. _____

A32 Compilers cannot check for logical errors in a program. _____

A33 Type checking is done during syntax analysis. _____

A34 Interpreted languages support Dynamic Typing. _____

A35 Interpreters do not generate any intermediate code. _____

A36 Symbol tables are also used during interactive debugging. _____

A37 In an interpreter, lexical analysis, parsing and type-checking are done just as in a compiler. _____

A38 In an interpreter, code is generated from the syntax tree. _____

A39 In an interpreter, the syntax tree is processed directly to evaluate expressions and execute statements. _____

A40 An interpreter may process the same portion of the syntax tree (ex. body of a loop) many times. _____

A41 Interpretation is typically slower than executing a compiled program. _____

A42 Developing an interpreter is usually simpler than developing a compiler. _____

A43 Compilation and interpretation may be not be combined to implement a programming language. _____

A44 Interpreter are better suited than compilers during program development. _____

A45 An interpreter works on a representation that is closer to the source code than is compiled code. _____

A46 The error messages can be more precise and informative (in general) in a compiler than in an interpreter. _____

A47   Compilers can detect runtime errors. _____

A48   Compilers cannot detect logical errors. _____

IOIOIOIOIOIOIOIOIOIOIOIOIOIOIOIOIOIOIOIOIOIOIOIOIOIOI

Fill-in the-blanks Questions

A1   The software which translates high-level language program into machine language program is known as _____

A2   The software which manages various resources and activities in a computer is known as the _____

A3   A(n) _____ provides facilities such as editing, compiling, running, and debugging during program development.

A4   A program which compiles without error(s) but terminates abnormally when run is said to have _____ error.

A5   A program which compiles without error(s) but produces incorrect result(s) is said to have _____ error.

A6   _____ strongly influenced the design of numerous imperative languages.

A7   The language used to describe another language is known as

_____

A8   _____ combines a number of independently compiled programs into an executable file.

A9   Languages in which a program specifies *how* a computation is to be done (*i.e.*, the steps of computation) are called _____ languages.

A10   Languages in which a program specifies *what* computation is to be done (without details of the steps) are called _____languages.

A11   A programming languages that supports more than one programming paradigm is known as _____ language.

A12 _____ was developed as a systems programming language for the development of UNIX.

A13 If each feature of a language can be used in conjunction with all other features, the features are said to be _____

A14 What a program looks like (or its structure) is called its _____

A15 The execution or meaning of each feature in a language is called its

_____

A16 Statement-oriented languages are also called _____ languages.

A17 The system program which combines separately compiled segments of a program into one executable is called a _____

A18 The process of replacing symbolic references or names of libraries with actual usable addresses in memory before running a program, is known as _____

A19 Relocation is done at compile time by the _____

A20 Relocation is done at runtime by the _____

A21 The _____ puts together all of the executable object files into memory for execution.

A22 The _____ is a program that works on the source code before the compilation.

A23 The macros in a program is expanded by the _____

A24 A program written in a high-level language is known as

_____

A25 The result of compiling a program is known as _____

A26 The result of combining several objects files into what the machine can execute is known as _____

A27 The rule or pattern specifying how a certain input sequence should be mapped to an output sequence according to a defined procedure is known as a _____

A28 The reference to a function in a file, which has been defined in a different file, will be resolved at _____ time.

A29 Sections of code that have to be included in many places in a program with little or no changes is known as _____ code.

A30 The most commonly used representation inside the computer is known as _____

A31 Unlike float or double data type, the _____ data type can store the exact decimal value (within the allowable range).

A32 Languages where type checking happens at run time are known as _____ typed languages.

A33 Languages that allow blocks to be nested are said to have

_____

A34 Separation of logical view of data from its underlying implementation is known as _____ abstraction.

A35 Separation of logical view of action from its underlying implementation is known as _____ abstraction.

A36 A program which does not compile is said to have _____ error(s).

A37 A program which compiles without error(s) but terminates abnormally when run is said to have _____ error.

A38 Separately compiled files of a program are combined into one executable by the _____

A39 External references are resolved at run time by a _____ linker.

A40 The intermediate code generated from the source code by Java compiler is known as _____

A41 The software that interprets (or compiles) Java bytecode is known as _____

A42 The data type which is not defined in terms of other types is known as _____

A43 The accuracy of the fractional part of a floating point (real) number is known as _____

A44 Just-in-time (JIT) compilation translates _____ code to _____ code.

A45 In most programming languages the two types of floating-point numbers supported are _____ and _____

A46 The database of a PROLOG program consists of _____ and _____

A47 In the _____ category of languages, 'what' needs to be computed is specified, and 'how' it is carried out is left to the system.

A48 The primary platform on which *C#* is used is the _____

IOIOIOIOIOIOIOIOIOIOIOIOIOIOIOIOIOIOIOIOIOIOIOIOIOI

Essay-type Questions

A1 List the major programming language paradigms.

A2 What is aliasing?

A3 Which is the most prevalent computer architecture, and what category of programming languages have been designed around them?

A4 Under what condition(s) is the compilation efficiency is preferred to the optimality of the object code produced?

A5 What is Just-in-time (JIT) compilation?

A6 What role does the symbol table play in a compiler?

A7 What does a linker do?

A8 What is the von Neumann bottleneck?

A9 What is a nonprocedural language?

A10 What was the first application for Java?

A11 For what application area is JavaScript most widely used?

A12 What does an XSLT processor do?

A13 What does a JSP (Java Server Pages) processor do?

A14 List the different language processers that a typical integrated software development environment would have.

A15 Give examples of syntax errors (in C, C++, Java, and similar languages).

A16 Give examples of run-time errors (in C, C++, Java, and similar languages).

A17 Give examples of logical errors (in C, C++, Java, and similar languages).

IOIOIOIOIOIOIOIOIOIOIOIOIOIOIOIOIOIOIOIOIOIOIOIOIOIOIOIOI

B. Names, Bindings, and Scopes

True/False Questions

B1   JavaScript does not support dynamic binding. _____

B2   The lifetime of static variables is the entire program execution time. _____

B3   The binding of a variable can change during the course of program under dynamic binding. _____

B4   The global variables are allocated on stack. _____

B5   Stack dynamic variables are bound to memory locations at compile time. _____

B6   In some languages, the type of a variable could change during the program execution. _____

B7   A static variable is allocated in the stack area of memory. _____

B8   An explicit heap dynamic variable needs a function or operator for its creation. _____

B9   The global variables in a program are *always* visible inside all subprograms. _____

B10   Dynamic binding can occur before the start of execution of the program. _____

B11   Dynamic allocation of memory is done by the compiler. _____

B12   A memory location could have multiple variable names referring to it. _____

B13   A variable name cannot refer to multiple memory locations at the same time. _____

B14   The lifetime of a stack–dynamic variable is the entire execution time of the program. _____

B15   Static variables are never allocated on stack. _____

B16 Dynamically allocated memory is always allocated in the stack area of memory. _____

B17 Dynamic scoping is based on the calling sequence of subprograms. _____

B18 A heap–dynamic variable must be explicitly deallocated in C++. _____

B19 In all languages, the scope of variables can be solely determined by the program text. _____

B20 Multiple variables of the same name but with different scopes can be used in the same program in C++. _____

B21 During run-time, an arbitrary number of memory cells need to be allocated for the parameters and local variables to support recursion. _____

B22 In most programming languages, the global variables are initialized. _____

B23 In most programming languages, the local variables are initialized. _____

B24 Using global variables instead of parameter passing increases execution speed. _____

B25 In a static array, the subscript ranges are not known before run time. _____

B26 In static binding, a variable can only be assigned values of the type specified at the time its declaration. _____

B27 In dynamic binding, a variable can only be assigned a value of a particular type during the execution of the program. _____

B28 The memory allocated to every variable is guaranteed to be at the same address for the entire duration of program execution. _____

B29 There could be cases where the declaration of a variable may not necessarily allocate the memory for it at compile time. _____

B30 Creation of dynamic data structures and objects cannot be done in static allocation. _____

B31 Static allocation would not work for recursive routines. _____

B32 All global variables are static variables. _____

B33 All static variables are global variables. _____

B34 Languages with dynamic binding are usually interpreted (than compiled). _____

B35 Local variables do not have default values. _____

B36 Local variables are initialized with default values when they are declared. _____

B37 It is possible for the type of a variable to be statically bound and it's storage to be dynamically bound. _____

B38 The type of a stack dynamic variable is not statically bound. _____

B39 The types of stack dynamic variables can change during execution. _____

B40 The type of an explicit heap dynamic variable is statically bound. _____

B41 The type of an implicit heap dynamic variable is statically bound. _____

B42 Static scoping is less efficient than dynamic scoping. _____

B43 The readability of code using static scoping is better than that using dynamic scoping. _____

B44 When a subprogram / method finishes and returns to the caller, all of the associated stack-dynamic variables are implicitly deallocated. _____

B45 Operators or methods are required for the allocation of stack–dynamic variables. _____

B46 Operators or methods are required for the allocation of explicit–heap dynamic variables. _____

B47 Operators or methods are required for the allocation of implicit–heap dynamic variables. _____

B48 Garbage collection is be used in the case of explicit heap–dynamic variables. _____

B49 There will be memory leaks in the use of static variables. _____

B50 There will be memory leaks with stack-dynamic variables. _____

B51 There will not be memory leaks with explicit heap dynamic variables. _____

B52 There will not be memory leaks with implicit heap dynamic variables. _____

B53 Under dynamic scoping, the scope can be determined at compile time. _____

B54 The type of an implicit heap-dynamic variable can change during runtime. _____

B55 The type of an explicit heap-dynamic variable can change during runtime. _____

B56 The type of a stack-dynamic variable can change during runtime. _____

B57 Dynamically allocated memory can sometimes have a lifetime equal to the entire program execution time. _____

B58 Memory leak is not a problem in languages using implicit deallocation. _____

B59 There is no difference between shallow copy and deep copy in the case of primitive data types. _____

B60 In a dynamically typed language, all type checking is done at runtime. _____

B61   Most dynamically typed languages are interpreted. _____

B62   In C++, a variable can be defined anywhere in the program where a statement can appear. _____

B63   In C++, namespaces cannot be nested within another. _____

B64   C++ supports dynamic binding of named constants to values. _____

B65   Java objects are explicit heap dynamic. _____

B66   Java provides no explicit operator or method to delete explicit heap dynamic variables. _____

B67   Java does not support dynamic binding of named constants to values. _____

B68   In Java, the packages are not hierarchical. _____

B69   In Java, there are no standalone subprograms. _____

IOIOIOIOIOIOIOIOIOIOIOIOIOIOIOIOIOIOIOIOIOIOIOIOIOIOIOIOIOI

Fill-in the-blanks Questions

B1   The _____ of a variable is the segment of the program within which it is declared and used.

B2   The region of the program in which a variable is declared and can be referred to (used) is called its _____.

B3   During a program's execution, the interval in which memory is assigned to a variable is known as the _____ of the variable.

B4   Under _____ or _____ scope, the visibility of variables can be determined based solely on the program text.

B5   It is possible to determine the scope of a variable by looking only at the program text in language using _____ or _____ scope.

B6   The listing of variable names and their types in a program is referred to as _____ declaration.

B7   The time during which a variable is bound to a specific memory location is called its _____

B8   A variable that is bound to a value once, and does not change thereafter, is known as _____

B9   A _____ binding occurs before run time and remains unchanged throughout program execution.

B10 The block (range of statements) in which a variable is visible, is referred to as its _____

B11 The collection of all variables that are visible in a statement is known as its _____

B12 The set of bindings in effect at a given point in a program is known as _____

B13 The (common) term used to denote the ability to select subprograms at run-time is _____ or _____

B14 _____ is an association between an entity and its attribute(s).

B15 _____ binding occurs before runtime.

B16 Assignment statement essentially binds _____ to _____

B17 _____ scope is based on calling sequences of subprograms.

B18 Under _____, the scope of a variable cannot be determined at compile time.

B19 _____ is the collection of the attributes of a variable.

B20 _____ is a special word in a programming language that cannot be used as a variable name.

B21 The _____ specifier indicates that a variable is defined elsewhere.

B22 A _____ is a variable that is bound to a value only once.

B23 In each of the following scenarios, at what stage/time does the binding gets defined?
  i.   Operator symbols to operations: _____

  ii. Floating point type to a representation: _____

  iii. Variables to (data) types (in C, C++, Java): _____

  iv. Static variables (in C, C++) to memory cells: _____

  v.   Non–static variables to memory cells: _____

B24 The L–*value* of a variable is its _____

B25 The R–*value* of a variable is its _____

B26 The six attributes of a variable are _____, _____, _____, _____, _____, and _____

B27 A variable which is visible in a statement (program unit), but not declared within the block where the statement appears is known as _____ variable.

B28 The allocation of all the data objects at compile time is known as _____ allocation.

B29 With explicit deallocation, absence of matching deallocation for every allocation leads to _____

B30 The number and size of all possible objects is known at compile time under _____ allocation.

B31 A variable that is bound to a memory cell during the entire execution time of the program is known as _____

B32 Recursive routines require _____ allocation.

B33 The association of an identifier in a program with a memory location (address) is called _____

B34 The automatic detection of the data type of an expression or a variable based on the context is known as _____

B35 A variable getting bound to a type when it is assigned a value is known as _____ binding.

B36 In _____ binding, a variable can be assigned a value of any type during the execution of the program.

B37 Languages with _____ binding are usually compiled (than interpreted).

B38 Two distinct (logical) areas of memory where dynamic variables are allocated are _____ and _____

B39 Memory that is allocated by OS before program starts execution is known as _____

B40 Variables which are allocated storage at runtime when execution reaches their declaration statement are known as _____ variables.

B41 Operators or constructor methods are required for the allocation of _____ variables.

B42 _____ variables are bound to storage at the time of execution of the operator / constructor methods.

B43 _____ variables are bound to storage at the time of assignment of a value.

B44 Garbage collection must be used in the case of _____ variables.

B45 The arguments of subprograms / methods are of type _____

B46 The types of stack dynamic variables are bound at _____ time.

B47 The type of _____ variable gets defined only when a value is assigned at runtime.

B48 The periodic, automatic reclamation by the system, of the dynamically allocated memory is known as _____

B49 A _____ binding can change during the execution of a program.

B50 In a _____ array the binding of subscript ranges can change any number of times during the array's life time.

B51 In C++ and Java, the variables declared in methods are, by default, of type _____

B52 The same name bound to multiple entities at the same time is known as _____

B53 Multiple names bound to the same entity at the same time is known as _____

B54 The same use of a variable could refer to any of several different declarations of that variable at run time with _____ scope.

B55 Use of a name referring to its declaration in the most recently called, but not-yet-terminated procedure is called _____ scope.

B56 In C++, by default all method binding is _____

B57 In Java, method binding, by default, is _____

B58 In Java, the keyword used for method declaration to indicate that the method cannot be overridden by subclasses is, _____

B59 In Java, a class that cannot be subclassed must be declared

_____

B60 In Java, if the method is declared final, _____ binding occurs.

IOIOIOIOIOIOIOIOIOIOIOIOIOIOIOIOIOIOIOIOIOIOIOIOIOI

Essay-type Questions

B1 List the (major) *entities* that are defined and manipulated programs of contemporary, procedural languages.

B2 In a *block–structured* language using *static scoping*, what is the rule for finding the correct declaration of the nonlocal variables?

B3   Briefly explain why dynamically typed languages are (usually) interpreted rather than compiled.

B4   How is the correct declaration of nonlocal variables found under *dynamic scoping*?

B5   What is an example of an error in a program which could result in exhaustion of memory for the *stack–dynamic* variables?

B6   What is an example of an error in a program which could result in exhaustion of memory for the *heap–dynamic* variables?

B7   Give examples of places in a program where the declared variables are *stack dynamic*.

B8   How are *explicit heap dynamic* variables deallocated and returned to the memory pool?

B9   Briefly describe the lifetimes of static, stack dynamic, explicit heap-dynamic, and implicit heap-dynamic variables.

IOIOIOIOIOIOIOIOIOIOIOIOIOIOIOIOIOIOIOIOIOIOIOIOIOIOIOIOI

C. Data Types

True/False Questions

C1   All integer values (within the machine representable range) can be represented without loss of precision. _____

C2   All floating point values (within the machine representable range) can be represented without loss of precision. _____

C3   A primitive data type can be defined in terms of other types. _____

C4   The limited dynamic strings of C/C++ do not require run–time descriptors. _____

C5   The values in a subrange type need not be contiguous. _____

C6   In all languages, an array should be homogeneous – consisting of elements of the same type. _____

C7   In the record type, all elements (fields) should be of the same type. _____

C8   Pointers require different memory sizes based on the data types of objects they point to. _____

C9   The members of a record type may reside in locations which are not adjacent. _____

C10 The elements of a heterogeneous array are always allocated consecutive memory locations. _____

C11 Java does not support the pointer type. _____

C12 C# supports both pointer and reference types. _____

C13 The contents of a pointer is a memory address. _____

C14 No arithmetic operation at all can be done on a pointer type. _____

C15 In every language, the array subscript has to be of integer type. _____

C16 The array index is always of type integer in all languages. _____

C17 The **int** datatype has different variations in C, C++, and Java. _____

C18 Several languages provide **string** as a primitive data type. _____

C19 There are some languages where the array subscript could be other than the integer type. _____

C20 The exact value of every floating point number within the allowed range can be stored in the computer. _____

C21 Typeless languages offer great flexibility for the programmer. _____

C22 Type checking in a language supporting dynamic type binding can be done at compile time. _____

C23 Type checking in languages does not necessarily reduce programmer errors. _____

C24 C++ is a type-safe language. _____

C25 The value of a variable of *pointer* type is any integer. _____

C26 The value of a variable of *pointer* type is a valid address. _____

C27 Primitive types are not reference types. _____

C28 Array types are reference types. _____

C29 In widening conversion, the magnitude of the converted value is not maintained. _____

C30 Integer to floating-point (widening) conversion will never result in loss of precision. _____

C31 Implicit type conversions (coercions) can be specified in programming language syntax. _____

C32 Implicit type conversions (coercions) can be specified in programming language semantics. _____

C33 Mixed mode expression may give incorrect results. _____

C34 Coercion (by itself) specified in a programming language always gives correct results in mixed-mode expressions. _____

C35 Implicit type conversion (coercion) provided in the language may never lead to logical errors. _____

C36 Casting may be necessary in addition to coercion for correct results. _____

C37 A type mismatch always results in a runtime error. _____

C38 For static arrays, the array subscripts are fixed at compile time. _____

C39 The type of a static variable is known before runtime. _____

C40 The type of a static variable can change during runtime. _____

C41 The type of a stack dynamic variable can change during run time. _____

C42 The type of an explicit heap–dynamic variable can change even after the allocation of storage. _____

C43 The type of an implicit heap–dynamic variable can change several times during execution. _____

C44 Heap dynamic variables do not have an explicit name when created. _____

C45 In Java, there are no operators or methods for deallocation of class instances. _____

C46 The size of a stack-dynamic array can change during runtime, after the array has been allocated. _____

C47 The subscript ranges of a stack-dynamic array can change during runtime, after the array has been allocated. _____

C48 The subscript ranges of a stack-dynamic array may not be known at compile time. _____

C49 The size of a stack-dynamic array may not be known at compile time. _____

C50 The size of a stack-dynamic array can be specified at run-time. _____

C51 Coercion (implicit type conversion) is always done at run-time in statically typed languages. _____

C52 Type checks are done only at compile time. _____

C53 Multidimensional arrays in C are arrays of arrays. _____

C54 The fields of a record are allocated consecutive memory locations. _____

C55 In C# class type checking can be specified to be done at run time rather than compile time. _____

C56 In Java, an array may contain only primitive types. _____

IOIOIOIOIOIOIOIOIOIOIOIOIOIOIOIOIOIOIOIOIOIOIOIOIOIOIOIOI

Fill-in the-blanks Questions

C1 _____ is the simplest of all data types.

C2 The type in which the range of all possible values is associated with the set of positive integers, is known as _____

C3 _____ is ordered contiguous subsequence of an ordinal type.

C4 _____ refers to a collection of data objects and a set of predefined operations on those objects.

C5 A _____ array is one in which the lengths of the rows need not be the same.

C6 _____ is a possibly heterogeneous aggregate of data elements where the individual members are identified by names.

C7 A _____ is a type whose members may store different type values at different times.

C8 _____ ensures that the operands of an operator are of compatible types.

C9 The application of an operator to an operand of an inappropriate type results in _____ error.

C10 In a _____ programming language most of the type (mismatch) errors are detected at compile time.

C11 A _____ language has stricter type checking rules at compile time,

C12 In C–based languages, explicit type conversions are called

_____

C13 A language is said to be _____ if an object cannot be used as an object of an unrelated type.

C14 _____ refers to accessing the value of a variable via the pointer to the variable.

C15 The value of a variable of *pointer* type is a(n) _____

C16 A _____ pointer is one that contains the address of heap–dynamic variable that has been deallocated.

C17 In _____ conversion, the converted type cannot include all of the values of the original type.

C18 The _____ conversion is usually safe (magnitude of the converted value is maintained).

C19 _____ is an unordered collection of data elements using key–value pairs.

C20 The underlying implementation of enumeration types is done using

_____

C21 Explicit type conversion in C–based languages is called _____

C22 Values of a(n) _____ type are represented by default as consecutive integers starting from zero.

C23 A _____ is a restriction on an existing type.

C24 Accessing an element of an array by name (key) is done in a(n) _____ array.

C25 Check for type safety done at compile time is known as _____

C26 Check for type safety done at runtime is known as _____

C27 Type checking is done at _____ time in statically typed languages.

C28 Type checking is done at runtime in _____ typed languages.

C29 The implicit/automatic type conversion of one data type to another, done by the compiler or interpreter, is known as _____

C30 The explicit conversion of a datatype to another type, done by the programmer, is known as _____

C31 Storage allocation for a static array is done at _____ time.

C32 The size of a _____ array can change during runtime, after the array has been allocated.

C33 The subscript ranges of a _____ array can change during runtime, after the array has been allocated.

C34 Multidimensional arrays in C are stored in _____ order.

C35 In multi-byte storage in a word, storing the least significant byte at the lowest address, called _____

C36 In multi-byte storage in a word, storing the least significant byte at the highest address, called _____

C37 The data with a value that is distinct from all legal data values, which is used to detect the end of the data, is known as _____

C38   In a static array, the subscript ranges are [statically?/dynamically?] _____ bound and storage allocation is done at _____ time.

C39   In a fixed stack-dynamic array, the subscript ranges are [statically?/dynamically?] _____ bound, and the allocation is done at _____ time.

C40   In _____ arrays, the binding of subscript ranges and storage allocation is done at run time, but do not change during execution.

C41   In _____ arrays, the binding of subscript ranges and storage allocation are dynamic and can change during execution.

IOIOIOIOIOIOIOIOIOIOIOIOIOIOIOIOIOIOIOIOIOIOIOIOIOIOI

Essay-type Questions

C1   What is a data type?

C2   What is the *type system* of a programming language?

C3   What is type checking?

C4   What is an abstract data type (ADT)?

C5   Give the formula for computing the starting byte address of the kth element of a 1–D array whose first element starts at address A, and each element is of size S.

C6   Consider a 2–D array A of N x M elements, each element of size S bytes. Assuming column-major order, by how many bytes offset will the element $A[1,2]$ be from $A[1,1]$ (the first element)?

C7   Consider a 2–D array A of N x M elements, each element of size S bytes. Assuming column-major order, the first element $A[1,1]$ is at address P, what is the starting byte address of element $A[k, l]$?

C8   Briefly describe the difference between *shallow* copy and *deep* copy.

C9   What is garbage collection?

C10   How is garbage collection done?

IOIOIOIOIOIOIOIOIOIOIOIOIOIOIOIOIOIOIOIOIOIOIOIOIOIOIOIOI

D. Expressions and Assignment Statements

True/False Questions

D1   All expressions will produce side effects. _____

D2   Evaluation of some expressions could change the value(s) of the components in the expression. _____

D3   Assignment statements produce side effects. _____

D4   The statements in functional languages do not have side effects. _____

D5   In Java, the sub-expressions are executed from left to right. _____

D6   In C++, the sub-expressions are executed in any order. _____

D7   In a short-circuit evaluation, the result of an expression can be determined without evaluating all of the sub-expressions. _____

D8   Arithmetic expressions can be the operands of relational expressions. _____

D9   Boolean expressions cannot be the operands of relational operators. _____

D10   All Boolean expressions can be the operands of relational expressions. _____

D11   Relational expressions can be the operands of Boolean operators. _____

D12   The result of evaluation of an arithmetic expression could be a Boolean value. _____

D13   The result of evaluation of a relational expression is always a Boolean value. _____

D14 A completely parenthesized expression could still have ambiguities in the order of evaluation. _____

D15 In a short–circuit evaluation, the complete expression is *never* evaluated. _____

D16 Short-circuit evaluation of arithmetic expression is usually no done. _____

D17 Short-circuit evaluation of any expression will always give the correct results. _____

D18 Control expressions must always be enclosed within parentheses. _____

D19 Assignments can be used as expressions in C–based languages. _____

D20 Assignment statements produce side effects. _____

D21 In most imperative programming languages, the operator precedence rules are the same. _____

D22 The exponentiation operator is provided by all C–family of languages. _____

D23 Programming language designer decides the operator precedence rules. _____

D24 Java guarantees left–to–right evaluation of operands. _____

D25 In widening conversion, the converted type can include all of the values of the original type. _____

D26 Widening conversions could result in loss of precision. _____

D27 The choice of full evaluation or short-circuit evaluation is usually specified in the programming language. _____

D28 The operators and subprograms which are overloaded may not operate on entirely distinct types. _____

D29 In the C++ statement **cout << num**, the function is **cout**. _____

D30   In C++, all of the operators can be overloaded. _____

D31   What are the values of the following expressions?

```
int a = 2, b = 3, c = 5;
```

i.   `a > b || c > b`   _____

ii. `b < a + 2 && c <= a + b`   _____

iii. `(b > c - a) || (a < c / b + 1)`   _____

iv. `b == b % c || a + b > c`   _____

v.   `(b <= c) && (b + c % a == 0)`   _____

IOIOIOIOIOIOIOIOIOIOIOIOIOIOIOIOIOIOIOIOIOIOIOIOIOIOIOIOI

Fill-in the-blanks Questions

D1   Expressions containing operators having operands of different types are known as _____ expressions.

D2   _____ and _____ rules govern the operator evaluation order in expressions.

D3   A _____ operator compares the values of its two operands.

D4   Determining the result of an expression without evaluating all of the parts of the expression is called _____

D5   Operators appearing between the two of their operands are called _____ operators.

D6   The normal precedence and associativity of operators can be overridden by using _____

D7   Computing the value of an expression without actually evaluating all components of the expression is known as _____

D8   The choice of full evaluation or short-circuit evaluation is usually left to the _____

D9   An operator having three operands is known as _____ operator.

D10   In the C++ statement **cout << num**, the function is _____

D11   _____ refers to multiple uses of an operator (based on different operand types).

D12   The same operator having different underlying operations based on the types of the operands at that time is known as

_____

IOIOIOIOIOIOIOIOIOIOIOIOIOIOIOIOIOIOIOIOIOIOIOIOIOIOIOI

Essay-type Questions

D1   In most programming languages, what do arithmetic expressions consist of?

D2   Give examples of two operators that are not associative.

D3   What are the values of **a** and **n** after the execution of the following statements?
```
a = 2; n = a++; a = n++; n = a++;
```

D4   What are the values of **a** and **n** after the execution of the following statements?
```
a = 2; n = a++; a = ++n; n = a++;
```

D5   What are the values of **a** and **n** after the execution of the following statements?
```
a = 2; n = ++a; a = n++; n = ++a;
```

D6   What are the values of **a** and **n** after the execution of the following statements?
```
a = 2; n = ++a; a = ++n; n = ++a;
```

D7   What is the difference between coercion and cast?

D8   What is an overloaded operator?

D9   What is short-circuit evaluation?

IOIOIOIOIOIOIOIOIOIOIOIOIOIOIOIOIOIOIOIOIOIOIOIOIOIOIOIOI

E. Statement-Level Control Structures

True/False Questions

E1   The **for** statement in C / C++ can be rewritten as a **while** loop. _____

E2   The **for**, **while**, and **do-while** loops do not have equivalent expressive power. _____

E3   Any of the **for**, **while**, and **do-while** loops can be transformed to the other having the same effect. _____

E4   The **do-while** loop always executes at least once. _____

E5   The **while** loop always executes at least once. _____

E6   The **for** loop always executes at least once. _____

E7   Multiple entries in a control structure is seldom used in practice. _____

E8   Multiple exits in a control structure is seldom used in practice. _____

E9   A *multiple selection control* cannot be simulated merely using multiple **if-else** statements. _____

E10 In a *pre-test loop*, the loop body is executed at least once. _____

E11 Theoretically, the **if** and **goto** statements are sufficient to express any needed control structure. _____

E12 The **break** statement inside an inner loop of a nested loop will pass control out of the all the nested loops to the statement outside of the outermost loop. _____

E13 The **break** statement inside a loop of a nested loop will pass control out of that loop and all of its inner loops. _____

E14   C–based languages do not provide multiple exits from control structures. _____

E15   Assignment statements always produce side effects. _____

E16   The *iterator* is essentially a function applied to the elements of a structured type. _____

E17   All the three expressions of the 'for' statement in C-style languages are optional. _____

E18   The **exp1** in **for (exp1; exp2; exp3)** can be executed more than once. _____

E19   The **exp1** in **for (exp1; exp2; exp3)** cannot consist of multiple statements. _____

E20   The **exp3** in **for (exp1; exp2; exp3)** can consist of multiple statements. _____

E21   The **continue** control statement transfers control to the the outermost loop. _____

E22   The **continue** control statement transfers control to the start of the loop, ignoring further statements after the **continue**. _____

IOIOIOIOIOIOIOIOIOIOIOIOIOIOIOIOIOIOIOIOIOIOIOIOIOI

Fill-in the-blanks Questions

E1   Statement that is used to modify the order of execution is known as _____ statement.

E2   A loop whose number of iterations is determined by the numeric value of a variable is known as _____ loop.

E3   A loop whose number of iterations is determined by the Boolean condition of an expression is known as _____ loop.

E4   In a _____ loop control structure, the loop body is executed at least once.

E5   It is more natural to use the _____ loop when the number of iterations is known *a priori* (before hand).

E6   The _____ control statement transfers control out of the smallest enclosing loop.

E7   The statement block in a _____ (or _____) control structure is executed at least once.

E8   The _____ control statement transfers control out of the smallest enclosing loop.

E9   The _____ construct allows the selection of one of a number of statements or statement groups.

E10   _____ causes a (compound) statement to be executed zero or more times.

E11   The _____ control statement transfers control to the control mechanism of the smallest enclosing loop.

E12   Theoretically, the only two control statements which can achieve the effect of any control flow in a program are the _____ and _____ statements.

E13   A control statement together with its associated block of statements is known as _____

E14   An optional **else** clause in an **if–then** [**–else**] statement resulting in nested conditionals being ambiguous is known as _____ problem.

E15   The condition that must be true before execution of a statement is called _____

E16   The condition that holds true after the execution of a statement is called _____

IOIOIOIOIOIOIOIOIOIOIOIOIOIOIOIOIOIOIOIOIOIOIOIOIOIOIOIOI

Essay-type Questions

E1 Do the **while**, **do-while**, and **for** loops have different expressive powers?

E2 What is the difference between **break** and **continue** statements (of C-family) of languages?

E3 What are the two broad categories of control statements?

E4 Briefly describe the two categories of loops.

E5 When is it beneficial have the **if** and multiple **else if** statements in a certain order?

IOIOIOIOIOIOIOIOIOIOIOIOIOIOIOIOIOIOIOIOIOIOIOIOIOIOIOIOI

F. Subprograms

True/False Questions

F1   Functions in most imperative languages can have either pass-by-value or pass-by-reference parameters. _____

F2   C allows return of arrays from functions. _____

F3   C allows return of functions from functions. _____

F4   Java and C# do not have functions. _____

F5   Global variables can never be passed as arguments to functions. _____

F6   In *pass-by-value*, it is possible for the called subprogram to change the values of the actual parameters of the calling subprogram. _____

F7   In the *out mode* (*pass by result*), the actual parameter is copied onto the formal parameter. _____

F8   A function can be defined in a file, but called in another function in a different file. _____

F9   It is possible to define multiple functions of the same name (in a file). _____

F10   In a recursive call of a subprogram, there are multiple instances of its activation record. _____

F11   The return address of a subprogram may not always be part of its activation record. _____

F12   Languages without stack dynamic variables cannot support recursion. _____

F13   No local variable declared inside a program can retain its value across multiple invocations. _____

F14   The static local variables of a subprogram are allocated on the stack (area of memory). _____

F15 The static local variables of a subprogram are not allocated/deallocated upon a function entry/exit. _____

F16 Static local variables of subprograms cannot support recursion. _____

F17 C++ makes use of C's linkers. _____

F18 Not all subclasses are subtypes. _____

F19 Not all subtypes are subclasses. _____

F20 Multidimensional arrays can never be passed as arguments. _____

F21 It is not possible in any language to decide the subprogram to be called at runtime.

F22 In C++ the parameter passing for arrays is call-by-value. _____

F23 In pass-by-value, it is possible for the called subprogram to change the values of the actual parameters of the calling subprogram. _____

F24 A function can return multiple results back to the calling subprogram. _____

F25 Some languages support passing subprograms as arguments to other subprograms. _____

F26 Subprogram exemplifies data abstraction. _____

F27 Aliasing can happen when parameters are passed by value. _____

F28 In C / C++, a function definition can have further nested function definitions. _____

F29 In the *out mode* (*pass by result*), the actual parameter is copied onto the formal parameter. _____

F30 In C / C++, the local variables of functions are always stack dynamic variables. _____

F31   In C / C++, the local variables of functions are always stack dynamic variables, *by default*. _____

F32   In C / C++, the lifetimes of local variables declared with **static** keyword extend beyond the time the function is active. _____

F33   In a recursive call of a subprogram, there are multiple instances of its activation record. _____

F34   C / C++ support both functions and procedures. _____

F35   In C / C++, a function defined in a file cannot be called in another function in a different file. _____

F36   In C/C++ functions can be passed as parameters. _____

F37   In C/C++ pointers to functions can be passed as parameters. _____

F38   The generic parameters of Java cannot be primitive types. _____

F39   Most imperative languages do not support returning arrays from functions. _____

F40   The exact type of operation in the case of overloaded operators in statically typed language may not always be determined at compile time. _____

F41   Different versions of overloaded subprograms could have the same protocol. _____

F42   In generic subprograms, the types of the formal parameters are bound to types of the actual parameters at compile time. _____

F43   The actions required for setting up a subprogram's call is less complicated than those of the subprogram's return. _____

F44   Allocation of memory for stack-dynamic variables requires explicit statements other than declarations. _____

F45   The format of the activation record (in most languages) is known at compile time. _____

F46   Subprogram parameters must always be passed via the stack. _____

IOI

Fill-in the-blanks Questions

F1   The _____ specifier indicates that a variable is defined elsewhere.

F2   Any two expressions in a program with the same value which can be substituted for one another, without affecting the program's behavior is known as _____

F3   Referential transparency is provided by programs in _____ languages.

F4   The number, type, order of parameters and the return type of a subprogram is collectively known as its _____

F5   In the *in mode* (*pass by value*) the _____ is copied into _____

F6   Parameter passing mechanism used for basic types (ex. integers, real, character) is _____

F7   In _____ parameter passing, the value of the actual parameter is copied to the parameters of the called subprogram.

F8   Parameter passing mechanism used for types other than the basic types is _____

F9   In _____ parameter passing, a pointer (or reference) to the object is passed to the called subprogram.

F10 The local variables in functions declared with the _____ keyword retain their values across function invocations.

F11 Operator precedence and associativity could be overridden by the use of _____

F12 The parameter passing mechanism used for arrays is _____

F13 Ambiguities about the corresponding **if** for an **else** in a nested **if-else** structures is called the _____ **else** problem.

F14 Data abstraction is routinely used in _____ (kind) of languages.

F15 The return type of C# event handler is _____

F16 The types of the parameters of a C# event handler are _____ and _____

F17 A function definition that is not bound to an identifier is known as _____

F18 Anonymous functions are most commonly supported in _____ (category) languages.

F19 A subprogram which takes parameters of different types on different activations is known as a _____ subprogram.

F20 Subprograms that do not require types of parameters to be specified, and can handle different types specified at runtime, are known as _____ subprograms.

F21 A _____ subprogram is one whose computation can be done on data of different types in different calls.

F22 In _____ subprograms, the types of the formal parameters are bound to types of the actual parameters at run time.

F23 The segment of the stack associated with each function call is called the _____

F24 Activation records are stored on _____

F25 Subprogram exemplifies _____ abstraction.

F26 The two fundamental kinds of subprograms are _____ and _____

F27 A _____ is a special subprogram that has multiple entry points.

F28 Subprograms that return a value are called _____, and those that do not return a value are called _____

F29 Local variables in the C family of languages are (by default) allocated as _____ variables.

F30 The parameter passing mechanism, where the values of the actual parameters are copied onto the formal parameters is called _____

F31 In most contemporary languages, parameter passing takes place via the _____ data structure.

F32 A(n) _____ subprogram has the same name as another subprogram in the same referencing environment.

F33 C / C++ does not allow _____ and _____ as return types in functions.

F34 A subprogram whose execution has begun but not yet terminated is said to be _____

F35 A function that takes one or more functions as arguments, or/and returns a function as its result, is known as _____ function.

F36 The evaluation of actual parameters (arguments) before calling the function is known as _____ evaluation.

F37 The evaluation of actual parameters (arguments) only if it is needed, or only to the extent needed is known as _____ evaluation.

F38 The actual parameters are not changed the _____ parameter passing.

F39 More than one formal parameter referring to the same object is known as _____

F40 Subprograms which retain (some or all) state information across invocations are known as _____

F41 For history-sensitive subprograms (some or all) local variables must be declared with the _____ keyword.

F42   A local variable of subprogram can retain its value across different invocations when declared with the keyword _____

F43   A subprogram and its referencing environment, are together known as, a _____

F44   When a subprogram returns, the values of the formal parameters are copied to the actual parameters in the _____ and _____ mode of parameter passing.

F45   The non-code part of a subprogram consisting of parameters, local variables, and return address (among a few other things) is collectively called _____

F46   The main items of a subprogram's activation record are _____, _____, and _____

F47   The addresses of the subprograms which are called are determined by the _____

F48   Languages which do not support _____ variables cannot support recursion.

F49   Subprogram parameters are (commonly) passed via _____ in RISC machines.

IOIOIOIOIOIOIOIOIOIOIOIOIOIOIOIOIOIOIOIOIOIOIOIOIOIOIOIOI

Essay-type Questions

F1   How is the exact type of operation determined in case of overloaded operators?

F2   In Ruby, when a return statement has multiple expressions, how are the values of the expressions returned?

F3   What is meant by subprograms being used as first-class objects?

F4   What is an overloaded subprogram?

F5   What are the main items in the activation record?

F6   What is the return address that is part of an activation record?

F7   What are the advantages and disadvantages of parameters passed only by reference?

F8   What is the *protocol* of a subprogram?

F9   Briefly describe *pass–by–value–result*.

F10   When would a global variable not be visible inside a subprogram?

F11   What are the disadvantages of pass-by-name parameter passing?

F12   Why are nested subprograms not allowed in several languages?

F13   What is meant by 'functions treated as first-class objects' in a programming language?

IOIOIOIOIOIOIOIOIOIOIOIOIOIOIOIOIOIOIOIOIOIOIOIOIOIOIOI

G. Object-Oriented Programming

True/False Questions

G1   A derived class cannot add variable(s) to those inherited from its base class. _____

G2   A derived class can add method(s) to those inherited from its base class. _____

G3   A derived class cannot modify the behavior of its inherited methods. _____

G4   A modified method of a derived class cannot have the same name as its parent's method. _____

G5   All of the variables of a base class will be visible in its derived classes. _____

G6   All of the methods of a base class may not be visible in its derived classes. _____

G7   Instance variables are associated with a class. _____

G8   Class variables are associated with a class. _____

G9   Class methods can perform operations only on the class. _____

G10   A graph is required to represent the relationship among several derived classes and the base classes in the case of single inheritance. _____

G11   A tree may not be adequate to represent the relationship among a derived class and the base classes in the case of multiple inheritance. _____

G12   All abstract classes must be completely independent. _____

G13   Private members of a base class are visible to its derived classes. _____

G14   An abstract class cannot be instantiated. _____

46

G15 An abstract class cannot be subclasses. _____

G16 The invocation of methods of object-oriented languages is slower than the invocation of subprograms of imperative languages. _____

G17 Operations to be applied to variables which could be bound to different types at runtime can be handled by static polymorphism. _____

G18 In static polymorphism, the actual method to be invoked can be resolved at compile time. _____

G19 In dynamic polymorphism, the actual method to be invoked cannot be resolved at compile time, but only at runtime. _____

G20 Method overloading is valid for methods not in the same class. _____

G21 Method overriding is valid for methods in different classes. _____

G22 In method overloading the signature (number and type of arguments) of the methods must be different. _____

G23 In method overriding the signature (number and type of arguments) of the methods could be different. _____

G24 In method overloading the return types of the methods must be the same. _____

G25 Overloaded functions/methods are in the same scope. _____

G26 Overridden functions/methods are in different scopes. _____

G27 Polymorphism is the process to define more than one body for functions/methods with same name.

G28 Method overriding can be viewed as polymorphism. _____

G29 Both method overloading and overriding can be viewed as providing polymorphism. _____

G30   In a single-inheritance object-oriented language, a class may have any number of base classes. _____

G31   In a single-inheritance object-oriented language, a class may have any number of superclasses. _____

G32   In a single-inheritance object-oriented language, a class may have any number of derived classes. _____

G33   The private components of an object are accessible to all objects of the same class. _____

G34   Polymorphism can be either static or dynamic. _____

G35   In C++, an abstract class may not have completely defined methods. _____

G36   In C++, a class need not have a parent class. _____

G37   C++ does not allow the abstract data types to be parameterized. _____

G38   C# structs do not support inheritance. _____

G39   In C++, class instances can only be heap dynamic (and not stack dynamic). _____

G40   In C++, the member functions of a class must defined within the class definition. _____

G41   Object-oriented languages such as C++ and Java do not support message passing. _____

G42   In Java, there is no explicit object deallocation. _____

G43   In C++, constructors and destructors can be defined for any class. _____

G44   In C++, method bindings can only be static. _____

G45   In C++, objects can only be heap dynamic. _____

G46   In C++, conversion from a value of a base type to a value of a derived type is allowed. _____

G47 C++ includes no predefined exceptions. _____

G48 In C++, the `catch` function can have only a single formal parameter. _____

G49 In C++, all of the instances of a class share a single copy of the member functions. _____

G50 In C++, each instance of a class has its own copy of the class data members. _____

G51 In C++, an abstract class contains at least one pure virtual function. _____

G52 In C++, a pure virtual function cannot be called. _____

G53 In C++, a function name can be overloaded even if the functions with that name have the same signature. _____

G54 An instance of a class is known as _____

G55 In C++, **cin** and **cout** are *__statements__* and **>>** and **<<** are _____

G56 In C++, objects (non-primitive types) cab be directly printed using the **<<** operator. _____

G57 In C++, the **<<** I/O operator cannot be overload to support printing the class objects. _____

G58 In C++, it is not possible to declare pointers to class objects. _____

G59 In C++, all class instances are heap dynamic. _____

G60 C++ has no encapsulation construct. _____

G61 C++ constructors cannot be overloaded. _____

G62 In C++, constructors and destructors do not have return types nor do they return values. _____

G63 In C++, references and pointers can be used on constructors and destructors. _____

G64 In C++, constructors can be declared with the keyword **virtual**.
_____

G65 In C++, constructors and destructors cannot be declared **static**, **const**, or **volatile**. _____

G66 C++ provides garbage collection (implicit reclamation of unreferenced storage). _____

G67 In C++, constructors and destructors obey the same access rules as member functions. _____

G68 In C++, storage allocated to objects can only be reclaimed by explicit call to **delete**. _____

G69 In C++, derived classes inherit constructors / destructors from their base classes. _____

G70 In C++, constructors can be overloaded. _____

G71 In C++, destructors can be overloaded. _____

G72 In C++, derived classes may call the constructor and destructor of base classes. _____

G73 In C++, non-inlined methods must be defined outside the class.
_____

G74 In Java, objects are accessed through reference variables. _____

G75 In Java, a class need not have a parent class. _____

G76 In Java, objects can be either stack dynamic or heap dynamic.
_____

G77 In Java, method bindings can only be dynamic. _____

G78 Java has friend functions and friend classes. _____

G79 In Java, all objects (class instances) are heap dynamic. _____

IOIOIOIOIOIOIOIOIOIOIOIOIOIOIOIOIOIOIOIOIOIOIOIOIOIOIOIOI

Fill-in the-blanks Questions

G1   In object-oriented languages the data abstraction construct is known as _____

G2   The variables and methods (subprograms) of a class are together called _____

G3   The members of a class that are visible only within the class are known as _____ members.

G4   The members of a class that are visible in its derived class are known as _____ members.

G5   In _____ languages, all computation is initiated via message passing.

G6   A class that is independent (not defined or derived from other classes) is known as _____

G7   A class (some of) whose components are inherited from some other class is known as _____

G8   A class from which a new class is derived is called _____ class.

G9   _____ is an instance of an abstract data type.

G10   A method of a class with only the protocol, but without a definition (body) is known as _____ method.

G11   A class with at least one abstract method is known as _____ class.

G12   Deriving a class from several base classes is called _____

G13   The number and type of arguments associated with a method are referred to as its _____

G14   In method _____, methods must have same name and different signature (number and type of arguments).

G15 In method _____, methods must have same name and same signature.

G16 Method _____ is considered compile time polymorphism.

G17 Method _____ is considered runtime polymorphism.

G18 The resolution of the appropriate operations to be applied to variables at run-time is known as _____ polymorphism.

G19 The functions and procedures that can operate upon the data members of a class are known as _____

G20 The collection of all methods of a class is known as the class's _____

G21 The calls to methods are sometimes referred to as _____

G22 The process of modifying a method in a derived class that has been inherited from a base class is known as _____

G23 The method of a derived class which is inherited from a base class that is modified is known as _____ method.

G24 The broad kinds of variables provided by classes are _____ variables and _____ variables.

G25 The broad kinds of methods provided by classes are _____ methods and _____ methods.

G26 The _____ variables are associated with objects.

G27 The _____ variables of a class store the state of an object of the class.

G28 There is only one copy of _____ variables for a class.

G29 _____ methods operate only on the objects of a class.

G30 _____ methods can perform operations both on the class and on objects of the class.

G31 A class derived from more than one base class is said to have _____ inheritance.

G32 The same method name overloaded with different type or number of parameters in same class is allowed in _____ polymorphism.

G33 In static polymorphism, the actual method to be invoked is resolved at _____ time.

G34 The same method overridden with same signature in different classes is allowed in _____ polymorphism.

G35 In _____ polymorphism, the actual method to be invoked can only be resolved at runtime.

G36 The facility which supports a collection of logically related code and data to be organized and independently compiled is known as _____

G37 A collection of classes and methods that are individually linked to an executing program, as needed during execution, is known as _____

G38 The association between a method and its class is contained in a table known as _____

G39 In static polymorphism, the multiple forms are resolved at _____ time.

G40 In C++, variables which are declared in another namespace can be accessed by using the _____ operator.

G41 In C++, special kind of parameter that can be used to pass a type as argument is known as _____

G42 In C++, a member of a class that can be redefined in its derived classes is known as a _____ member.

G43 In C++, a class that declares or inherits a virtual function is known as a _____ class.

G44 In C++, late binding of a method is achieved by the use of the _____ keyword in a method's declaration.

G45 The objects of a(n) _____ class cannot be modified.

G46 In C++, data abstraction is provided by _____

G47 In C++, the access specifiers are _____, _____ and _____

G48 In C++, the member function of a class which has no definition is known as _____ function.

G49 In C++, a function not defined in a class, but which can access the non-public members of a class is known as _____ function.

G50 C++ supports parameterized ADTs through its _____ classes.

G51 In C++, heap allocated objects are explicitly deallocated using the _____ method.

G52 In C++, _____ subprograms or classes have full access to private data and operations of the class.

G53 In C++, the implicit conversion of a value of a derived class to a value of its base class is called ___ or _____ conversion.

G54 In C++, a _____ component is accessible to any user of the class.

G55 In C++, _____ component is accessible within the class as well as within a class derived from it.

G56 In C++, a _____ component is accessible only within the class.

G57 In C++, the inlining of methods eliminates the cost of _____

G58 In Java, only _____ types are not objects.

G59 Java objects are allocated on the _____

G60 In Java, all classes are descendants of the _____ class.

G61 In Java, a method that is defined to be _____ cannot be overridden in any descendant class.

IOIOIOIOIOIOIOIOIOIOIOIOIOIOIOIOIOIOIOIOIOIOIOIOIOIOI

Essay-type Questions

G1   What is a class?

G2   What are the similarities between subprograms (of procedural languages) and methods (of object-oriented languages)?

G3   What are the differences between subprograms (of procedural languages) and methods (of object-oriented languages)?

G4   Why cannot the actual method to be invoked in dynamic polymorphism be determined at compile time?

G5   What is a major problem with multiple inheritance?

G6   What are the benefits provided by inheritance in ADTs (Abstract Data Types)?

IOIOIOIOIOIOIOIOIOIOIOIOIOIOIOIOIOIOIOIOIOIOIOIOIOIOIOI

H. Exception Handling

True/False Questions

H1   An exception is a run-time condition. _____

H2   All exceptions are errors. _____

H3   All errors detectable by compilers are detected by the hardware. _____

H4   Checks for array subscript (index) going out of bounds is provided by all languages. _____

H5   Exceptions cannot be handled in languages that do not have built-in exception handling facility. _____

H6   In C++, an exception handler may re-throw the exception to be intercepted by another handler. _____

H7   In C++, there is no direct way to access the object thrown during an exception that is caught by a **catch(...)** block. _____

H8   In C++, the programmer cannot implement one's own **unexpected()** function. _____

H9   In C++, the **unexpected()** function (when called on unspecified exception), can further throw an exception. _____

H10 In C++, a **terminate()** function can never return to its caller. _____

H11 In C++, the inherited subprograms in the derived class cannot be overridden by redefining the subprogram. _____

H12 In C++, a programmer defined function can be called when an exception is not handled. _____

H13 In C++, all thrown errors can be caught and successfully dealt with by a catch block. _____

H14 C++ exceptions cannot be user-defined class. _____

H15 In C++, any object can be thrown, including the object that caused the exception. _____

H16 In C++, the `catch(...)` must be the last catch block. _____

H17 In C++, `try` block must be accompanied by one or more `catch` blocks. _____

H18 Java provides some default exception handlers. _____

H19 In Java, a method must declare all exceptions that it can possibly throw. _____

H20 In Java, unchecked exceptions can be thrown by any method. _____

H21 In Java, user programs cannot define their own exception classes. _____

IOIOIOIOIOIOIOIOIOIOIOIOIOIOIOIOIOIOIOIOIOIOIOIOIOIOI

Fill-in the-blanks Questions

H1 During program execution, a condition requiring special processing is known as _____

H2 Run-time anomalies or abnormal conditions encountered by a program during its execution are known as _____

H3 The special processing required of an exception condition is commonly known as _____

H4 In C, the _____ facility enables defining additional points within the program that the exception handler can return to.

H5 In C++, the _____ statement causes an exception to be raised.

H6   In C++, the _____ block identifies the scope of a sequence of statements for which exception handlers are active.

H7   In C++, the _____ block contains the exception handler.

H8   In C++, the decision made at compile-time whether to call the inherited subprogram or the newly defined subprogram is called

_____

H9   In C++, a _____ block implements an exception handler.

H10 In C++, the _____ must be the last catch block.

H11 In C++, the _____ clause handles the exception when no catch is used.

H12 In C++, the _____ handler catches all thrown exceptions that have not been caught by a previous catch block.

H13 In C++, the default implementation of unexpected() calls

_____

H14 In C++, a thrown exception that is not listed in the exception specification, the library function that is called to handle it is

_____

H15 In C++, a **catch** block follows immediately after a _____ statement or immediately after another _____ block.

H16 In C++, an exception handler is implemented in a _____ block.

H17 In Java, the two categories of exception are _____ and

_____

H18 In Java, unchecked exceptions are of class _____ and _____ and their descendants.

H19 In Java, all exceptions are objects of classes that are descendants of the _____ class.

H20 In Java, the super class of all exceptions is the _____ class.

H21 In Java, the two predefined exception classes (subclasses of **Throwable**) are _____ and _____

H22 In Java, errors that are thrown by the run-time system are associated with the _____ exception class and its descendants.

H23 In Java, the keywords related to exception handling are _____, _____, _____, _____ and _____

H24 In Java, the statements that may throw exceptions are in the _____ block.

H25 In Java, the keyword for declaring an exception is _____

H26 In Java, the keyword for (manually) throwing an exception is _____

H27 In Java, if an exception occurs, it is caught and handled (processed) by the _____ block.

H28 In Java, the operator used to create instance of an exception is _____

IOIOIOIOIOIOIOIOIOIOIOIOIOIOIOIOIOIOIOIOIOIOIOIOIOIOIOI

Essay-type Questions

H1 Give examples of exceptions.

H2 List some advantages of support for exception handling in a programming language.

H3 Give the C++ keywords along with their purpose for handling exceptions.

H4 In C++, where are the allowable objects that a function can catch declared?

H5 In C++, what are the types of objects that can be caught during exception?

H6 In C++, list the scenarios when **terminate()** is called.

H7   What are the C++ language constructs for handling exceptions?

H8   Briefly describe the control flow in the **catch** blocks in C++.

H9   Describe the structure and function of a **catch** block in Java.

H10   Describe the exception handling constructs in C++.

H11   Describe the exception handling constructs in Java.

H12   In Java, which part of code gets executed whether exception is caught or not?

IOIOIOIOIOIOIOIOIOIOIOIOIOIOIOIOIOIOIOIOIOIOIOIOIOIOIOIOIOI

I. Languages and Features

True/False Questions

I1   The variables in BASIC do not have explicit types. _____

I2   In Smalltalk, all objects are allocated on the heap. _____

I3   Smalltalk has an explicit deallocation operation to delete objects. _____

I4   COBOL supports dynamic data structures. _____

I5   COBOL supports recursion. _____

I6   In Ada, casts have the syntax of function calls. _____

I7   Ada packages cannot be compiled separately. _____

I8   Type checks and array bounds are not done in C. _____

I9   In C/C++, the pre-processor directives cannot be used to create macros. _____

I10   The '*' operator in C/C++ has operation(s) other than multiplication. _____

I11   In C, storage for a variable of non-primitive type must always be explicitly allocated by the use of some 'allocation' operator. _____

I12   In C, I/O functions are not supported by the basic language constructs. _____

I13   In C, string is not a basic (primitive) datatype. _____

I14   C does not have (explicit) Boolean data type. _____

I15   C supports (explicit) String data type. _____

I16   C/C++ does not have array-bounds checks. _____

I17   In C/C++, files containing one or more subprograms can be independently compiled. _____

I18   C++ has garbage collection mechanism. _____

I19   C++ provides no operations on enumeration types. _____

I20   In C#, the pre-processor directives can be used to create macros. _____

I21   In C#, the pre-processor directives can be used for conditional compilation. _____

I22   Java is a type-safe language. _____

I23   Java bytecode can only be compiled, and not interpreted, into native code at run time. _____

I24   In Java, a class should always contain a no-arg constructor. _____

I25   In Java's Math class, all methods are static. _____

I26   In Java, the constructors must always be public. _____

I27   In Java, the constructors of a class may be protected. _____

I28   Java does not have array-bounds checks. _____

I29   Java does not have a pre-processor. _____

I30   Java does not support macros. _____

I31   Java has no pointer data type. _____

I32   In Java, a default constructor is automatically provided if no constructors are explicitly declared in the class. _____

I33   In Java, at least one constructor must always be defined explicitly for a class. _____

I34   In Java, every class provides a default constructor. _____

I35   In Java, the default constructor is a no-arg constructor. _____

I36   In Java, multiple constructors cannot be defined in a class. _____

I37   In Java, constructors do not have a return type (including void).
_____

I38   In Java, constructors must have the same name as the class itself.
_____

I39   In Java, whenever a variable of non-primitive type is declared, a block of memory of the required size is allocated. _____

I40   In Java, the methods or data members declared as *protected* are accessible within same package but not in sub classes in different package. _____

I41   In Java, the static method exists even before an object of a defined class is created. _____

I42   In Java, more than one variable-length parameter may be specified in a method. _____

I43   In Java, the variable-length parameter specified in a method must be the last parameter. _____

I44   In Java, the return type of a method could be a variable-length parameter. _____

I45   In Java, a non-static method can be called from a static method.
_____

I46   In Java, a static method can be accessed from a non-static method.
_____

I47   Java byte code does not hide machine-specific details. _____

I48   In Java, call-by-value is not used. _____

I49   A garbage collection mechanism is supported by the Java Virtual Machine (JVM). _____

I50   In Ruby, all instance variables are private by default, and that cannot be changed by the programmer. _____

I51   Ruby supports return of more than one value from a method.
_____

I52   Ruby supports multiple inheritance. _____

I53   In Ruby, classes are dynamic (members can be added / deleted / changed during execution). _____

I54   In Ruby, the type of an object can be statically determined. _____

I55   In Ruby, even arithmetic, relational, and assignment operators are implemented as methods. _____

I56   In Ruby, there is no type checking of parameters. _____

I57   In Ruby, the formal parameters are typeless. _____

I58   In Python, the types of formal parameters must be specified. _____

I59   In Python, there is no type checking of parameters. _____

I60   The long integer type of Python can have unlimited length. _____

I61   Tuples in Python are mutable. _____

IOIOIOIOIOIOIOIOIOIOIOIOIOIOIOIOIOIOIOIOIOIOIOIOIOIOIOIOIOI

Fill-in the-blanks Questions

I1   The language in which all operators have equal precedence, and associate right-to-left is _____

I2   The language which uses a large range of special graphic symbols is _____

I3   The central datatype in APL is _____

I4   The central data structure in Scheme is _____

I5   The single data type of Prolog is _____

I6   Record type was first introduced in the _____ language.

I7   The language with the most reserved words is _____

I8   The encapsulation construct in Ada is called _____

I9   In Ada related declarations of types, variables, and subprograms which are grouped together is known as _____

I10   In _____, array subscripts / indices need not be contiguous.

I11   An early language developed for AI (artificial intelligence) applications is _____

I12   The unary '*' operator in C/C++ is used for the _____ operation.

I13   In C++, _____ functions facilitate access to private members of a class.

I14   In C++, the operators **new** and **delete** manage _____ storage.

I15   In C++, (the default) pointer whose value is the address of the object is _____

I16   In C#, a variable can have dynamic binding if declared with the reserved word _____

I17   In _____ language a variable with a **var** declaration must have an initial value.

I18   In Java, whenever a variable of non-primitive type is declared, a(n) _____ is allocated.

I19   In Java, instance variables that are visible only in the class where they are defined are called _____

I20   In Java, instance variables that are visible everywhere are called _____

I21   In Java, instance variables that are visible in the class where they are defined and in all of the subclasses is called _____

I22   In Java, a method that is associated with a specific class is known as _____ method.

I23   In Java, a method that is associated with an object of a class is known as _____ or _____ method.

I24   In Java, a _____ is a collection of classes.

I25   Associative arrays of Python are known as _____

I26   The base class of all exception classes in Python is _____

I27   In _____ language, the arithmetic, relational, and assignment operators are implemented as methods.

I28   In Ruby, exceptions are explicitly raised with the _____ method.

I29   Every exception class in Ruby has two methods, namely _____ and _____

I30   All objects in Ruby are allocated on the _____

I31   In Ruby, every exception clause has methods named _____ and _____

I32   In Perl, scalar variable name begins with ___, array name begins with ___, and hash structure name begins with ___

I33   Associative arrays of Perl are known as _____

I34   A variable name must begin with a special character in the _____ programming language.

IOIOIOIOIOIOIOIOIOIOIOIOIOIOIOIOIOIOIOIOIOIOIOIOIOIOIOIOIOIOI

Essay-type Questions

I1   What is the role of modules in Fortran?

I2   What is the role of packages in Ada?

I3   What is the role of C++ namespace?

I4   What is the role of Java package?

I5   What are Python's modules and packages?

I6   What are Java's primitive types?

I7   What are the different native data structures supported in Python?

I8   What are the roles of operators in Ruby?

I9   Give examples of languages which do not require declaration of variables before use.

I10   Give examples of languages which require declaration of variables before use.

I11   Give examples of languages which allow variable declarations to be anywhere a statement can be.

I12   Give examples of languages which do not allow declaration of a variable in a nested block to have the same name as a variable in the enclosing block.

I13   Give examples of languages which do not have reserved keywords.

I14   Give examples of languages which support dynamic scoping.

I15   Give examples of languages which support closures.

I16   Give examples of languages which require the label of `goto` statements to be within the same procedure.

I17   Give examples of languages which have compound assignment operators (ex. +=).

I18   Give examples of languages which have (some) prefix operators.

I19   Give examples of languages where all operators are prefix operators.

I20   Give examples of languages which support conditional expressions (using '?' and ':' operators).

I21   Give examples of languages which do not have multiple-selection statement.

I22   Give examples of languages which have multiple-selection statement.

I23   Give examples of languages which support use of arithmetic expressions as control expressions in conditional statements.

I24   Give examples of languages which support arrays of heterogeneous element types.

I25   Give examples of languages which support array initializations at the time of allocation.

I26   Give examples of languages which specify array index range checks.

I27   Give examples of languages which support array slices.

I28   Give examples of languages which support expanding and shrinking arrays (which have already been allocated).

I29   Give examples of languages which are (commonly) interpreted (not compiled).

I30   Give examples of languages which store characters in 16–bit Unicode (UCS–2).

I31   Give examples of languages which support **union** type.

I32   Give examples of languages which support sets (unordered collections of distinct values from some ordinal type called base type).

I33   Give examples of languages which support **complex** numbers as built-in datatype.

I34   Give examples of languages which support **complex** numbers via **libraries.**

I35   Give examples of languages which provide **string** as a primitive type.

I36   Give examples of languages which support **decimal** datatype.

I37   Give examples of languages which have two sets of logical operators (**&&, and** ; **| |, or**).

I38   Give examples of languages which support enumeration types.

I39   Give examples of languages which support type inference (automatic detection of datatype based on context of use).

I40   Give examples of languages which support regular expressions.

I41   Give examples of languages which support nesting of classes.

I42   Give examples of pure object-oriented languages.

I43   Give examples of languages which support multiple inheritance.

I44   Give examples of languages (pure object-oriented or with object-oriented support) which do not directly support multiple inheritance.

I45   Give examples of languages which support user-defined overloaded operators.

I46   Give examples of languages which support subroutines with polymorphic parameters.

I47   Give examples of languages which support parameters having default values (if no actual argument is passed during call).

I48   Give examples of languages which support only stack-dynamic local variables in the methods.

I49   Give examples of languages which support user-defined aggregate data types (ex. arrays, structures).

I50   Give examples of languages in which methods are treated as objects and passed as parameters and returned from functions.

I51   Give examples of languages that support naming encapsulations.

I52   Give examples of languages which support concurrency.

I53   Give examples of imperative languages which support object-oriented features.

I54   Give examples of languages which have built-in garbage collection.

I55   Give examples of languages which do not allow coercions in expressions.

I56   Give examples of languages in which only widening assignment coercions are done.

I57 Give examples of languages which support implicit type conversions.

I58 Give examples of languages which support explicit type conversions.

I59 Give examples of languages which support negative indices (subscripts).

I60 Give examples of languages which support character indices (subscripts).

I61 Give examples of languages which allow the else-part of a conditional be optional.

I62 Give examples of object–oriented languages.

I63 Give examples of scripting languages.

I64 Give examples of logic programming languages.

I65 Give examples of early languages developed for AI (artificial intelligence) applications.

I66 Give examples of functional languages.

I67 Give examples of languages which use short circuit evaluation of Boolean expressions.

I68 Give examples of languages which do not do parameter type checking.

I69 Give examples of languages which allow return of multiple values from functions/methods.

I70 Give examples of languages which allow return values of any type from functions/methods.

I71 Give examples of languages where the assignment statement produces a result and can be used as an operand.

I72 Give examples of languages which allow multiple-target multiple-source assignments

I73   Give examples of languages which support *out mode* parameters.

I74   Give examples of languages which do not have the **goto** control structure.

I75   Give examples of languages in which any numeric type value can be assigned to any numeric type variable.

I76   Give examples of languages which support imperative, object-oriented, and functional paradigms.

I77   Give examples of functional languages in which functions are treated as first-class objects.

I78   Give examples of scripting languages in which functions are treated as first-class objects.

I79   Give examples of languages in which functions (not the values returned) can be assigned to variables.

I80   Give examples of languages which have predefined overloaded subprograms.

I81   Give examples of languages in which control expressions can be arithmetic.

I82   Give examples of languages in which control expression must be Boolean.

I83   Give examples of languages which have labeled versions of **continue.**

I84   Give examples of languages which allow mixed-mode expressions.

I85   Give examples of languages which do not allow mixed-mode expressions.

I86   Give examples of procedural (imperative) languages.

I87   Give examples of languages that support pointers.

I88   Give examples of languages that support pointer arithmetic.

I89 Give examples of languages which support dynamic type binding of variables.

I90 Give examples of languages where there is no limit on the length of a variable name, and all characters are significant.

I91 Give examples of languages which require explicit declaration of variable type.

I92 Give examples of languages which support implicit declaration of variable type.

I93 Give examples of languages which perform type checks at compile time.

I94 Give examples of languages which perform type checks at runtime.

I95 Give examples of languages which support heap-dynamic arrays.

I96 Give examples of languages which support nested subprogram definitions.

I97 Give examples of languages which do not support nested subprogram definitions.

I98 Give examples of languages which support associative arrays.

I99 Give examples of languages which support record types.

I100 Give examples of languages which support strong typing.

I101 Give examples of languages which require all variables to have a declared type.

I102 ave built-in pattern matching operations.

I103 Give examples of languages which support pattern matching operations via libraries.

I104 Give examples of languages which support strings of fixed lengths (static lengths).

I105 Give examples of languages which support strings of varying lengths with no maximum.

I106 Give examples of languages which support reference types.

I107 Give examples of languages which have built-in exponentiation operator.

I108 Give examples of languages which do not have exponentiation operator.

I109 Give examples of languages which support operator overloading.

I110 Give examples of languages which support polymorphism.

I111 Give examples of languages which support parameterized ADTs.

I112 Give examples of languages which support implicit iterators over elements of a container object.

I113 Give examples of languages which support dynamic scoping (in addition to static scoping) of variables.

I114 Give examples of languages which have built-in support for exception handling.

IOIOIOIOIOIOIOIOIOIOIOIOIOIOIOIOIOIOIOIOIOIOIOIOIOIOIOI

J. Compilers

True/False Questions

J1   For an unambiguous grammar, the leftmost and the rightmost derivations produce different parse trees. _____

J2   All syntax rules of a context free language can be specified in BNF. _____

J3   The syntax analyzer is also commonly called the parser. _____

J4   A terminal symbol could be on the LHS of a production rule of a grammar. _____

J5   BNF is a meta–language commonly used to describe the syntax of a programming language. _____

J6   The lexical analyzer is also commonly called the parser. _____

J7   Interpreted code generally runs faster than compiled code. _____

J8   Lexical analyzers are usually developed as a function called by the syntax analyzer. _____

J9   A non-terminal can appear on the RHS (Right Hand Side) of its definition. _____

J10   A terminal symbol could be on the LHS of a production rule of a grammar. _____

J11   *Java Bytecode* is the machine code which can be executed by the bare hardware. _____

J12   A sentence in a (programming) language could consist of non–terminal symbols. _____

J13   Code optimization is a mandatory step in all compilers. _____

J14   The descriptive power of EBNF is more than that of the corresponding BNF. _____

J15 The nonterminal on the LHS of a production cannot appear on its RHS. _____

J16 There could be more than one RHS for a given LHS of a production. _____

J17 All syntax rules of a context free language can be specified in BNF. _____

J18 Attribute grammars are used to specify the static semantics. _____

J19 The lexical analyzer (scanner) can be (in most cases) automatically generated based on the regular expressions of the lexemes. _____

J20 The output of the syntax analyzer is the input to the lexical analyzer. _____

J21 Lexical analysis (scanning) precedes syntax analysis (parsing). _____

J22 The output of the syntax analyzer is the input to the lexical analyzer. _____

J23 EBNF is best suited for (implementing) recursive–descent parsers. _____

J24 A recursive–descent parser produces a parse tree in bottom–up order. _____

J25 Left recursion is not a problem for LR (bottom up) parsers. _____

J26 There are ways of modifying a grammar to remove left recursion. _____

J27 The parsing table of an LR parser can easily be produced manually (by hand). _____

J28 The top of the parse stack of an LR parser always contains a state number. _____

J29 Each of the different types of tokens (ex. numbers, variables, keywords) are described by its own regular expression. _____

J30 A left-linear grammar cannot be converted to a right-linear grammar. _____

J31 A language is regular if and only if it is accepted by finite automata. _____

J32 If a grammar has more than one leftmost (or rightmost) derivation the grammar is ambiguous. _____

J33 The intermediary nodes of the syntax tree are the tokens found by the lexical analysis. _____

J34 The leaves of the syntax tree read from left to right yields the same sequence as in the input text. _____

J35 The language $a^{20}b^{15}$ is regular. _____

J36 The language $\{a^n b^n \mid n \geq 0\}$ is regular. _____

J37 The language $a^* b^*$ is regular. _____

J38 The matching parentheses cannot be described by regular expressions. _____

J39 Every regular a language can be expressed by a grammar. _____

J40 Every grammar describes a regular language. _____

J41 LR parser (Left-to-right, Rightmost derivation) can recognize any deterministic context-free language in linear-bounded time. _____

J42 Canonical LR parser is no more powerful than LALR parser. _____

J43 Code optimization is carried out on the intermediate code rather than on the machine code. _____

J44 All finite languages are regular. _____

J45 All regular languages are finite. _____

J46 A programming language which supports recursion can be implemented with static storage allocation. _____

J47 Context-free grammars are adequate to describe all of the syntax of (most) programming languages. _____

J48 The parsing algorithms of commercial compilers for programming languages have complexities less than O(N^3). _____

J49 Every regular grammar is LL(1). _____

J50 Every regular set has a LR(1) grammar. _____

J51 Left-recursive grammar is not suitable for predictive-parsing. _____

J52 Context Free languages are accepted by finite automata. _____

J53 LR grammars are a restricted class of BNF grammars. _____

J54 If a context free grammar G is ambiguous, the language L(G) generated by grammar G may or may not be ambiguous. _____

J55 It is always possible to convert any ambiguous CFG to an unambiguous CFG. _____

J56 Some ambiguous CFG can be converted to unambiguous CFG. _____

J57 There always exists an unambiguous CFG corresponding to unambiguous context-free language (CFL). _____

J58 Deterministic CFL may sometimes be ambiguous. _____

J59 Lexical analyzer is a finite automaton to recognize regular expressions. _____

J60 An ambiguous grammar cannot be parsed by an LR(k) parser for any k. _____

J61 An LR(k) grammar ($k > 1$) can be transformed into an LR(1) grammar. _____

J62 LR(k) parser cannot recognize all deterministic context-free languages. _____

J63 Symbol table can be used for checking type compatibility. _____

J64   A bottom-up parser generates the left-most derivation. _____

J65   A bottom-up parser generates the right-most derivation in reverse. _____

J66   It is generally easier to compile declarative languages into efficient machine code than imperative languages. _____

J67   Lexical analysis can detect invalid / unexpected structure in programs. _____

J68   No production in a LL(1) grammar can be left-recursive. _____

J69   All lexemes (tokens) can be described by regular expressions. _____

J70   Lexical analysis must necessarily be recursive in order to handle nested parentheses. _____

J71   Balanced parenthesis cannot be described by regular expressions. _____

J72   Lexical analyzers do not need to have any knowledge of the grammar of a language for their correct operation. _____

J73   Finite State Machines may never have unlimited number of states. _____

J74   A successful parse of a program indicates that it is semantically correct. _____

J75   Syntax analysis cannot handle type checking and type conversions. _____

J76   There are only a finite number of unambiguous non-LR(1) grammars. _____

J77   The root of the parse tree is the start symbol of derivation. _____

J78   LL parser can parse an ambiguous grammar. _____

J79   SLR parser cannot parse an ambiguous grammar. _____

J80   LR parser can parse an ambiguous grammar. _____

J81 The number of states of the SLR parser for a grammar has necessarily the same number of states as the LALR parser for the same grammar. _____

J82 Syntax trees are a form of intermediate representation. _____

J83 Syntax trees are commonly used during syntax and semantic analysis. _____

J84 LALR parser is more powerful than SLR parser. _____

J85 An operator precedence parser is a bottom-up parser that handles an operator-precedence grammar. _____

J86 High-level language programs can be translated to different intermediate representations. _____

J87 Compilers typically generate the executable with zero as the starting address. _____

J88 Semantic analysis is done before parsing. _____

J89 Optimization on the intermediate representation can be done before code generation. _____

J90 Peephole optimization is usually done on the generated instructions. _____

J91 Peephole optimization can never be done on the intermediate representation. _____

J92 With the use of optimizing compiler, the order of the statements as executed may be different from the order in the source code. _____

J93 The parse tree does not captures the associativity and the precedence of the operators. _____

J94 A top-down parser cannot handle left recursive productions. _____

J95 Some compilers produce only intermediate-level code instead of machine code. _____

J96 In some systems, some parts of a program are compiled to machine code, and some parts to intermediate code. _____

J97 The intermediate code produced by a compiler is always interpreted at runtime. _____

J98 It is never the case that in *any* system parts of a program are compiled to machine code, and parts are compiled to intermediate code. _____

J99 Compiled code tends to be bigger than intermediate code. _____

J100 Compilation of code into an intermediate language facilitates portability by hiding machine-specific details. _____

J101 Left recursion is not a problem for LR parsers. _____

J102 Unambiguous context-free grammars always generate a Deterministic context-free language (CFL). _____

J103 Not every context-free language is deterministic. _____

J104 Deterministic context-free languages (DCFL) are a proper subset of context-free languages. _____

J105 Deterministic context-free languages (DCFLs) form a proper subset of unambiguous context-free languages (CFLs). _____

J106 Some Deterministic Context Free Languages can be ambiguous. _____

J107 Every unambiguous Context-Free Language (CFL) is accepted by a deterministic Pushdown Automaton (PDA). _____

J108 Unambiguous grammars always generate deterministic Context-Free Languages (CFLs). _____

J109 Any language generated by a Context-Free Grammar (CFG) can be recognized by a Pushdown Automaton (PDA). _____

J110 Any language recognized by a Pushdown Automaton (PDA) can be generated by a Context-Free Grammar (CFG). _____

J111 Every CFG has a corresponding PDA. _____

J112 Every CFG has a corresponding deterministic PDA. _____

J113 Any (regular) grammar constructed from a DFA will be LL(0). _____

J114 In bottom-up parsing, the string to the right of the handle contains only terminals. _____

J115 Type checking is done before parsing. _____

J116 Type checking is done in the syntax analysis (parsing) phase of the compiler. _____

J117 Type checking is done in syntax directed translation. _____

J118 Checks for ensuring variable declarations before use can be described in the extended Backus–Naur form. _____

J119 There exist some languages whose compilers can produce the object code in a single pass (of a compilation unit / source code). _____

J120 Hashing cannot be used a method of organizing the symbol table. _____

J121 Any context-free grammar can be modified in order to be parsable by the recursive-descent parser. _____

J122 There is guarantee that any context-free grammar can be modified to be parsable by table-driven methods. _____

J123 Every language that can be described by a regular expression can also be described by a grammar. _____

J124 Every language that can be described by a grammar, can also be described by a regular expression. _____

J125 There are algorithms to remove both left recursion and common prefixes in grammars. _____

J126 A language may be LL(1) even though the grammar used to describe it is not. _____

J127 All grammars can be rewritten to allow LL(1) parsing. _____

J128 LL parser belongs to the class of bottom-up parsers. _____

J129 LL parser does not use backtracking. _____

J130 LR parsers belong to the class of bottom-up parsers. _____

J131 LR parsers accept a much larger class of grammars than LL parsers. _____

J132 Predictive parsers use backtracking. _____

J133 Recursive descent parsers do not use backtracking. _____

J134 Recursive descent parsers work bottom-up. _____

J135 Languages defined by regular grammars are a proper subset of the context-free languages. _____

J136 A non-recursive Context-Free Grammar (CFG) can generate infinite number of strings. _____

J137 Bottom-up parsing technique uses rightmost derivation. _____

J138 There is no backtracking in shift-reduce parsers. _____

J139 Leftmost and rightmost derivations could lead to different parse trees even in unambiguous grammar. _____

J140 The LR parser can recognize any deterministic context-free language in linear time. _____

J141 The memory requirements of LR parser is about the same as those of SLR and LALR parsers. _____

J142 The LALR parser is more powerful (in terms of language-recognition power) than the SLR parser. _____

J143 The LALR parser is less powerful (in terms of language-recognition power) than the CLR parser. _____

J144 LR parsers are no more powerful (in terms of the range of grammars handled) than LL parsers. _____

J145 LALR parser does not need backtracking. _____

J146 LR parsers are deterministic. _____

J147 LR parser requires backtracking. _____

J148 LR parsers produce a parse in linear time. _____

J149 Bottom-up parsers can handle grammars that top-down parsers cannot handle. _____

J150 Bottom-up parsers build the parse tree from left to right. _____

J151 Leaves of a parse tree are the tokens generated by the lexical analyzer. _____

J152 Leaves of an abstract syntax tree are the tokens generated by the lexical analyzer. _____

J153 The abstract syntax tree must be very closely tied to the grammar. _____

J154 A token can have only one associated lexeme. _____

J155 For LR, LALR, and SLR parsers, the basic state machine is the same. _____

J156 The parsing tables of LR, LALR, and SLR parsers are the same. _____

J157 In left factoring, the common prefix must be a terminal. _____

J158 In left factoring, the common prefix must be a non-terminal. _____

J159 Left factoring need not be done on grammars in order to be handled by LR parsers. _____

J160 LR parsers can handle grammars with left recursion. _____

J161 Left factoring need not be done on grammars in order to be handled by predictive parsers. _____

J162 Top-down parsers cannot handle left recursion in grammars.
_____

J163 Predictive parsers can handle grammars with left recursion.
_____

J164 All ambiguous grammars have multiple choices of production for a nonterminal, causing conflicts during parsing. _____

J165 Unambiguous grammars never cause conflicts (for the choice of production for a nonterminal) during parsing. _____

J166 In predictive (top-down) parsing, there can be nonterminals to the left of the rewritten non-terminals. _____

J167 There is no backtracking in an LL(1) parser. _____

J168 A non-recursive Context-Free Grammar (CFG) can generate an infinite number of strings. _____

J169 Look-ahead of input symbols in LR parser avoids backtracking (or guessing). _____

J170 A shift-reduce parser can parse the input text in one pass without backtracking. _____

J171 The parsing table entries (cells) for a deterministic parser cannot have multiple, alternative actions. _____

J172 The parse stack of the LR parser contains only grammar symbols.
_____

J173 The top entry in the parse stack of an LR parser is always a state symbol. _____

J174 Right linear grammar can be translated to a DFA (Deterministic Finite Automaton). _____

J175 Left linear grammar cannot be translated to a DFA (Deterministic Finite Automaton). _____

IOIOIOIOIOIOIOIOIOIOIOIOIOIOIOIOIOIOIOIOIOIOIOIOIOIOIOIOIOI

Fill-in the-blanks Questions

J1 _____ is the set of all strings over an alphabet.

J2 _____ specifies rules for forming valid sentences.

J3 Every string of symbols in a derivation is called a _____

J4 _____ enable additions to CFGs to carry some semantic info on parse tree nodes.

J5 An alphabet is a set of _____

J6 The set of all strings over an alphabet is called the _____

J7 The rules for forming valid sentences in a language is specified by its _____

J8 The smallest meaningful unit in the string representing a program is called _____

J9 _____ refers to the category of the smallest meaningful unit (lexeme) in a program.

J10 The _____ breaks down the string representing a program into meaningful units.

J11 The process of converting a sequence of characters in the source code to tokens is known as _____

J12 _____ refers to the structure of program (units).

J13 _____ refers to the meanings of program (units).

J14 The set of symbols and rules for generating a regular language is known as _____

J15 The compact algebraic notation which describes the set of all strings that are generated by a regular grammar is known as

_____

J16 The set of all strings generated by a regular grammar is known as

_____

J17 _____ is the class of languages that can be generated by regular grammars / described by regular expressions / recognized by finite automata.

J18 The mechanism which recognizes/accepts the language generated by regular grammar is a _____

J19 _____ is the universally used meta–language to describe the syntax of programming languages.

J20 The output of the lexical analysis phase of compiler is a set of _____

J21 The input to the syntax analyzer are the _____ which are output from the _____

J22 The output of the syntax analysis phase of compiler is the _____

J23 _____ is a hierarchical (graphical) representation of a derivation using grammar rules.

J24 _____ grammar can describe both the syntax and *static* semantics of a language.

J25 _____ is a language generator.

J26 _____ is a language recognizer.

J27 *BNF* stands for _____

J28 The forms of the tokens of programming languages can be described by _____ grammars.

J29 The syntax of programming languages can be described by _____ grammars.

J30 _____ are the input to the syntax analyzer.

J31 Computing the attribute values of a parse tree is sometimes called _____ the parse tree.

J32 _____ denote the meaning of the expressions, statements, and program units.

J33 The stage of compilation that is often optional is the _____ phase.

J34 _____ is the mathematical machine on which both top–down and bottom–up parsers are based.

J35 The mechanism which recognizes/accepts the language generated by Context-Free Grammar is known as _____

J36 The two primary operations (actions) of an LR parser are _____ and _____

J37 The keywords of a language are recognized during the _____ phase of the compiler.

J38 In a compiler, the _____ contains information about variables and their attributes.

J39 A _____ parser builds the parse tree starting with the start nonterminal.

J40 Recursive descent parsing belongs to the class of _____ parsing.

J41 Bottom-up parsing is also known as _____ parsing.

J42 Code optimizing transformations can be performed at _____ code and _____ code levels.

J43 The automaton associated with BNF (Backus-Naur Form) grammar is the _____ automaton.

J44 A Context-Free Language (CFL) is generated by a _____ grammar and is recognized/accepted by a _____

J45 _____ generates lexical analyzers from the input consisting of regular expression description of tokens of a language.

J46 _____ produces syntax analyzers (parsers) from input based on grammatical description of programming language (a context-free grammar).

J47 A context-free grammar that has at most one nonterminal in the RHS of each of its productions is known as a _____

J48　A grammar in which the non-terminal in RHS of the productions is at the left end is known as _____ grammar.

J49　While parsing an input string, a top-down parser uses _____ derivation.

J50　The outcome of the syntax analysis (parsing) stage is the _____

J51　The leaves of the syntax tree are the _____ (found by the lexical analysis).

J52　A Context-Free Grammar that has at most one non-terminal in the right hand side of each of its productions is known as _____ grammar.

J53　The LR class of parsers in order of increasing power are _____, _____, _____

J54　The two parts of the parse table of LR parser are _____ part and _____ part.

J55　For an entry in the Action part of the parse table, the row index is a _____ and the column index is a _____

J56　For an entry in the Goto part of the parse table, the row index is a _____ and the column index is a _____

J57　The possible entries in the Action part of the LR parse table are _____, _____, _____ and _____

J58　The entries in the Goto part of the LR parse table are the _____

J59　The most commonly used data structure to maintain the state of a shift-reduce parser is _____

J60　The top entry in the parse stack of an LR parser is always _____

J61　The process of using a compiler to compile itself is known as _____

J62 _____ is a program that takes a set of token definitions (each consisting of a regular expression and a token name) and generates a lexical analyzer.

J63 _____ enables code reuse/libraries, parallel development and collaboration.

J64 The _____ adds annotations to the abstract syntax tree produced by the parser.

J65 _____ parsing starts at the highest level of the parse tree and works down the parse tree by using the rules of grammar.

J66 _____ parsing starts at the lowest level of the parse tree and works up the parse tree by using the rules of grammar.

J67 _____ parsing attempts to find the leftmost derivations for an input string.

J68 _____ parsing reduces the input string to the start symbol of a grammar.

J69 LL parsers belong to the class of _____ parsers.

J70 LR parsers belong to the class of _____ parsers.

J71 A compiler that recompiles only those portions of a program that have been modified is known as _____ compiler.

J72 The _____ compiler avoids wasteful recompiling of entire source code, where only a small portion of the code is changed.

J73 The technique where the intermediate representation of source code is compiled to native machine code at runtime is known as _____

J74 An interpreter for a programming language written in that language itself is known as _____

J75 The process which allows a compiler to produce different executable programs based on parameters that are provided during compilation _____

J76   The process of applying the production rules of a grammar for obtaining the input string of the language is known as _____

J77   Any initial part of a string w including the empty string and all of the symbols of w is known as the _____ of w.

J78   The number of prefixes of a string of length N is _____

J79   A _____ of a string is what remains of the string after a prefix has been taken off.

J80   A subsequence of a string is obtained by deleting any number of symbols from anywhere in the string. The subsequences of **abc** are

_____

J81   The number of subsequences of a string of length N (with distinct symbols) is _____

J82   Errors that are not detected by the syntax analysis phase of the compiler are checked by the _____ phase of the compiler.

J83   Type checking is done in the _____ phase (part) of the compiler.

J84   The _____ parser uses leftmost derivation while parsing an input string.

J85   A compiler that translates a high-level language into another high-level language is called a _____ translator.

J86   A compiler that runs on platform (hardware/OS) and generates executable code for another platform (hardware/OS) is known as

_____

J87   Semantic analysis is also known as _____

J88   _____ translation works by adding actions to the productions in a context-free grammar.

J89   The front-end of a typical compiler consists of _____, _____, _____, and _____ phases.

J90 The back-end of a typical compiler consists of _____ and _____ phases.

J91 _____ attempts to replace short sequences of instructions with a single, more efficient instruction.

J92 A grammar which leads to a situation where there is more than one correct parse tree for a given expression (statement) is known as _____

J93 A production of grammar where the leftmost variable of its RHS is same as non-terminal of its LHS is known as _____

J94 A recursive descent parser is (usually) implemented based directly on _____

J95 The correct RHS to be selected from among more than one RHS in the reduction process of a bottom–up parser is known as _____

J96 The leaf nodes of a parse tree correspond to the _____ of the grammar.

J97 The interior nodes of a parse tree correspond to the _____ of the grammar.

J98 _____ traversal of the parse tree gives the original input string.

J99 Parse tree is also known as _____ tree or _____ tree.

J100 The interior nodes of the syntax tree represent _____

J101 The leaf nodes of the syntax tree represent _____ (arguments of operations).

J102 A production of the form $A \rightarrow B$, where both A and B are single non-terminals is known as _____

J103 Each application of a production rule in reverse in bottom-up parsing is known as _____

J104 In bottom-up parsing, the RHS of a rule to which a reduction is applied is known as _____

J105 Top-Down parsing starts with the _____ and applies the production rules by replacing _____ of the rule with _____ of the rule until the _____ is derived.

J106 Bottom-Up parsing starts with the _____, and applies the production rules by replacing _____ of the rule with the _____ until the _____ is derived.

J107 Three commonly used techniques for capturing the meaning (describing semantics) of a program are _____, _____ and _____ semantics.

J108 Axiomatic semantics is based on _____.

J109 Denotational semantics is based on _____.

J110 _____ semantics is based on descriptions of state changes as the program executes.

J111 The data structure mapping each symbol in the source code to associated information such as location, type and scope is known as the _____

J112 Type information can be stored in either the _____ or in the _____

J113 The commonly used data structures for the symbol table are _____, _____, _____, and _____

J114 LL(1) parser cannot handle a grammar that has _____ or _____ (in RHS of productions).

J115 _____ parsing starts with the sentence (input string of terminals), and arrives at the start symbol.

J116 In the parsing process of a bottom-up parser, the symbols corresponding to the _____ side of a production rule are replaced with the _____ side of the rule.

J117 Top-down parsing starts with the _____ and ends with the _____

J118 The most common techniques for rewriting grammars to make them amenable for LL(1) parsing are _____ and _____

J119 LR parsers belong to the category of _____ parsers.

J120 LR(1) parser is also known as _____ parser.

J121 In a CFG, a production in the form $X \rightarrow aX$ where 'a' is a string of terminals is called a _____ production.

J122 In a CFG, a production in the form $X \rightarrow Xa$ where 'a' is a string of terminals is called a _____ production.

J123 The top-down parsing is completed when it arrives at _____

J124 The bottom-up parsing is completed when it arrives the _____

J125 For lexical analysis, specifications are traditionally written using _____

J126 The _____ performs syntax analysis at the lowest level of program structure.

J127 The algorithms used in the parsers of compilers used in practice have a complexity (in terms of N, the length of string to be parsed) of _____

J128 A bottom-up parsing starts with the _____

J129 A bottom-up parsing (assuming no errors) ends with the _____

J130 _____ parsing starts at the leaves of the parse tree, and works back to the root.

J131 Bottom-up parsing starts with the _____, and finishes when the _____ is reached.

J132 At every step in the reduction, the bottom-up parser replaces the _____ of a production with the _____ of that production.

J133 _____ parser applies the production rules in reverse.

J134 The main decision in a _____ parser is the choice of production rule to apply.

J135 All of the leaves of a parse tree are the _____

J136 All of the internal (non-leaf) nodes of a parse tree are the

_____

J137 _____ is a compact way to describe a language that can be accepted by a finite-state machine.

J138 The repeated trials of syntax analyzer to determine the correct production among multiple rules of the same production is known as _____

J139 A state (an entry in the parsing table) of an SLR parsing table requesting both a shift action and a reduce action is known as _____ conflict.

J140 A state (an entry in the parsing table) of an SLR parsing table requesting two or more different reduce actions is known as _____ conflict.

J141 The condition where there are several choices of production for a nonterminal during parsing is known _____

J142 In predictive (top-down) parsing, there are only _____ to the left of the rewritten non-terminals.

J143 Replacing the part of input string that matches right-hand side (RHS) of a production with the nonterminal of the LHS of that rule is done in _____ parsing methods.

J144 The process of parsing is completed when the parser finishes at the start symbol starting from the input string in _____ parsing.

J145 In the RHS of any production of _____ grammar, the terminal symbol must precede the non-terminals.

J146 _____ is done for a context-free grammar which fails the pairwise disjointness test.

J147 During compilation, the process of recognizing, evaluating, and reusing constant expressions is known as _____ or

_____

J148 During compilation, replacing expensive operations (ex. multiplication) with equivalent but less expensive operations (ex. additions) is known as _____

J149 Statements / expressions inside loops which do not change across iterations are known as _____

J150 During compilation, moving loop-invariant code outside the body of a loop is known as _____ or _____

J151 During compilation, inserting the code of function definition at the places of function calls, is known as _____

J152 During compilation, detection of variables that are never used, and skipping operating on them, is known as _____

J153 During compilation, exchanging inner loops with outer loops in order to improve the locality of array references, is known as

_____

J154 During compilation, breaking a loop into multiple loops over the same index range, with parts of the body of the original loop (to improve locality of reference), is known as _____ or

_____

J155 During compilation, eliminating loop by taking code from inside the loop and repeating it, is known as _____

IOIOIOIOIOIOIOIOIOIOIOIOIOIOIOIOIOIOIOIOIOIOIOIOIOIOIOIOI

Essay-type Questions

J1 Show the Chomsky Hierarchy of language classes, and their corresponding grammars, and the automata for the recognition of the languages.

J2   Give the connections among regular grammar, regular language, regular expression, and finite automata.

J3   Give the connections among context-free grammar, context-free language, BNF notation, and push-down automata.

J4   List all the lexemes in the statement: `C = (F-32)/1.8;`

J5   What are the components of a context-free grammar (CFG)?

J6   What is the format of a production in a CFG?

J7   What are the main parts of a compiler?

J8   Give examples of static semantics which are not handled any CFG (Context Free Grammar).

J9   List three semantics description mechanisms.

J10   When is a rule in a grammar called recursive?

J11   What is a derivation?

J12   What is a sentential form?

J13   What is leftmost (rightmost) derivation?

J14   Consider the following grammar:
```
<assign> → <id> = <expr>
<id>     → A | B | C
<expr>   → <id> + <expr>
           | <id> * <expr>
                 | ( <expr> )
                 | <id>
```
Show a parse tree and leftmost derivation for the following statements:
    a. `A = A + (B * ( C + A ) )`
    b. `A = A * ( B + C )`

J15   Show that the following grammar is ambiguous.
```
<S>   → <A>
<A>   → <A> + <A> | <id>
<id> → a | b | c
```

J16   Consider the following grammar:

```
S → aS | bS | a
```

Give the derivation for: **abaaba**

J17 Consider the following grammar. Show the parse tree and leftmost derivation of the sentence "**bbaab**"

```
S → AaBb
A → Ab | b
B → aB | a
```

J18 Consider the following grammar.

```
S → AaBb
A → Ab | b
B → aB | a
```

Show the parse tree and left-most derivation for the sentence "**baaab**" using the above grammar.

Show the leftmost derivation of the sentence "**bbbaaab**" using the above grammar.

J19 Consider the following production rules:
```
S → aS | bS | a | b
```

Which of the following are valid sentences generated by applying the production rules? (Show by √ or X)
 1. **aaabb**
 2. **ababab**
 3. **aabbaa**
 4. **baabbb**
 5. **bbbaaba**

J20 Consider the following production rules:
```
S → aRb
R → aR | Rb | a | b
```

Which of the following are valid sentences generated by applying the production rules? (Show by √ or X)
 1. **aaaab**
 2. **aabaa**

3. **ababb**
4. **abbbb**
5. **aabbbb**
6. **baaa**
7. **aabb**

J21   Consider the following grammar:
```
S → aAb | bBA
A → a | aAB
B → aB | b
```

Starting from the following sentential forms, show sequence of sentential forms and the parse tree produced by bottom-up parsing going up to the start symbol of the grammar.
1. **aaAbb**
2. **bBab**

J22   Give the regular expression for the language generated by the following grammar.
```
S → aAb | aBb
A → aA | a
B → bB | b
```

J23   What is the language generated by the following grammar.
```
S → aSa | B
B → bB | b
```

J24   Give the regular expression for the language generated by the following grammar.
```
S → aRa
R → aR | Rb | a | b
```

J25   Give regular expression for the language generated by the following grammar
```
S → AaBb
A → Ab | b
B → aB | a
```

J26   Give the regular expression for the language generated by the following production rules.
```
S → aS | bS | a | b
```

J27 Give the regular expression for the language generated by the following production rules:
```
S → aRb
R → aR | Rb | a | b
```

J28 Write a grammar for the language consisting of the strings:
$a^n b^{2n}$, $n > 0$.

J29 Give the parse tree and rightmost derivation of string "**abab**" from grammar G given by S → SS | aSb | bSa | ε

J30 Convert the following BNF to EBNF.

```
<stmt_list> → <stmt> | <stmt>; <stmt_list>
<stmt> → <var> = <expr>
<var> → A | B | C
<expr> → <var> + <var> | <var> - <var> |<var>
```

J31 Describe the language generated by the following grammar:
```
S → A | B | a | b
A → bA | a
B → aB | b
```

J32 Give the notation and description for the language accepted by the grammar: S → aSb | ε.

J33 Give the CFG for the language $\{a^n b^m \mid m > n\}$.

J34 A *binary number* is any string of '0's and '1's, of length at least 1. Give the productions to generate binary numbers.

J35 Write the productions of a grammar to generate the language:
$\{a^N b a b^N, N \geq 0\}$

J36 Show that the following grammar is ambiguous by finding a string that has two different syntax trees (**id** is treated as a terminal). Show the syntax trees.
```
A → - A
A → A - id
A → id
```

J37 Briefly describe how compilation of code into an intermediate language facilitates portability across hardware.

J38   What are the properties of an operator precedence grammar?

J39   What is the most common approach of implementing a deterministic finite-state machine (FSM)?

J40   What do 'L' and 'L' denote in LL parser?

J41   In an LL(k) grammar, what does the 'k' denote?

J42   What do 'L' and 'R' denote in LR parser?

J43   What are the (common) LR parser variants?

J44   What do the letters in 'S', 'L', 'R' in SLR parsing denote?

J45   What are non-LL(1) languages?

J46   What are the primary tasks of a lexical analyzer?

J47   Briefly outline the three approaches to building a lexical analyzer.

J48   What are the two distinct goals of syntax analysis?

J49   Why do parsing algorithms used in commercial compilers work on only a subset of all grammars?

J50   What are the two grammar characteristics that prohibit them from being used as the basis for a top–down parser?

J51   Briefly describe the pairwise disjointness test.

J52   What is pairwise disjointness test?

J53   Which production rule will fail the pairwise disjointness test?

J54   What is a simple phrase of a sentential form?

J55   What is the handle of a sentential form?

J56   What is a recursive descent parser?

J57   Outline the working of LR parser.

J58   What are the advantages of LR parsers?

J59   A top-down parser builds the parse tree from the top down, starting with the start symbol. There are two types of top down Parsers:

1. Top down parsers with backtracking
2. Top down parsers without backtracking

J60   What are the main actions in top-down parsing?

J61   What is predictive parsing?

J62   What are the main actions of a Shift-Reduce parser?

J63   Give the Shift-Reduce Parsing steps for the following grammar for the input string **abbcde**.

```
S  →  aABe
A  →  Abc | b
B  →  d
```

J64   Outline the benefits of LR Parsing.

J65   What is a top-down parser?

J66   What is the requirement of an operator precedence parser?

J67   Give example of a language that context-free, but not deterministic context-free.

J68   Give the structure of production rules of a regular grammar.

J69   What is three address code?

J70   Why is turning off the optimizer option of compiler recommended when using a source debugger?

J71   What is the basic condition for predictive parsing?

J72   What is the main difference between parse tree and syntax tree?

J73   What is left factoring?

J74   When is left factoring used?

J75   Give an example of left factoring.

J76   Perform left factoring on the grammar production:

A → aAB | aAc | aBc

J77   List some of the limitations of syntax analyzer that are handled by the semantic analyzer.

J78   Briefly describe the difference between grammar and parser of a programming language.

J79   Give an outline of the operation of a bottom-up parser.

IOIOIOIOIOIOIOIOIOIOIOIOIOIOIOIOIOIOIOIOIOIOIOIOIOIOIOIOIOI

Answers

A. Preliminaries and Overview

True/False Questions

A1   In the early years of high–level language programming readability
was not an important issue. ***True***
[In the early years, the programs were highly specialized, and developed and used by a
closed community of users and readability was not a pressing issue]

A2   Readability is not important in modern languages. ***False***
[With ever increasing sizes of real-world software systems, the maintenance costs constitute
over 2/3ʳᵈ of the total system cost. Readability is important in reducing the maintenance
costs, via faster identification and fixing of bugs, making updates/enhancements faster, etc.]

A3   Increasing writability/flexibility of a language (generally) leads to
reduced reliability, and vice versa. ***True***

A4   Strict controls in a language to increase reliability leads to
(relatively) higher cost of execution. ***True***
[Strict controls require more checks than usual, and lead to increased execution times and
cost]

A5   Code from another file cannot be included in another file without
explicitly copying it. ***False***
[Preprocessor commands (ex. #include) can be used which includes the contents of files
needed for compilation, without the user explicitly coping them]

A6   The most prevalent category of programming languages is the
nonprocedural languages. ***False***

A7   An object file contains the symbol table of the identifiers that are
externally visible. ***True***

A8   The imperative languages are highly influenced by the von
Neumann architecture. ***True***

A9   The assignment statement is not required in pure functional
languages. ***True***

A10 There are no languages without reserved words. ***False***
[PL/I and Fortran do not have reserved words]

A11 The reference to a function in a file, which has been defined in a different file, can be resolved at compile time. *False*
[These are resolved at link time]

A12 Dynamically typed languages are never strongly typed. *False*
[Smalltalk, Perl, Ruby, Python are dynamically typed, and they perform type checks at runtime]

A13 A computer without the appropriate floating-point hardware can still perform floating-point operations using floating-point instructions emulator. *True*

A14 Scripting languages are usually interpreted languages. *True*

A15 Many contemporary languages do not allow nested subprograms. *True*

A16 Pattern matching using regular expressions is not supported in any language. *False*
[Perl has built-in support for regular expressions. Java, Python, Ruby provide support via libraries]

A17 Inlining a function or method makes it more efficient. *True*
[Inlining avoids the overhead of function call which involves saving/restoring activation records on/from the stack, and transfer of controls]

A18 Inlined function or method eliminates the cost of linkage. *True*

A19 The macros in a program are expanded during the compilation process. *False*
[Macros are expanded by the preprocessor which is not part of the compiler. The preprocessing is done before the start of compilation]

A20 Translating a high-level language program to intermediate code helps portability. *True*
[The compiler for the language can generate the same intermediate code, irrespective of the target hardware/processor. The language virtual machine for a particular processor can interpret or compile the intermediate code to the machine code for the particular processor]

A21 There is no guarantee that an arbitrary real numbers (floating-point) will have the exact values inside the computer. *True*
[This due to the fact that the word-length and the representation mechanism cannot accommodate all the possible numbers in the wide range]

A22 A floating-point variable can store the exact value within the allowable range of representation. *False*

A23 The range of integer values is much less than those of real numbers (floating point, double precision) in computer representation. *True*

A24 The result of compiling a program is always directly executable by the machine. *False*
[In general, the compilers produce the object code which are not directly executable. These need to be further linked to other object files (ex. libraries) to produce the executable code or machine code. Some language processors (ex. Java) compile the source to an intermediate code, which is not executable by the machine]

A25 An integer variable can store the exact value within the allowable range of representation. *True*

A26 Interpreters are less portable than compilers. *False*

A27 Code optimization is mandatory step in all compilers. *False*

A28 Interpreters are slower than compilers. *True*

A29 Interpreters do not require symbol table during interpretation. *False*
[Interpreters also need access to the types and memory locations (among other things) of the variables, which are stored in the symbol table]

A30 Hybrid implementation systems are slower than pure interpreters. *False*

A31 Just-in-time (JIT) compilation translates the source code to the (executable) machine code. *False*
[JIT translates the source code to an object code of intermediate format (resembling assembly language). Only those object code modules which are required during execution are compiled into machine code]

A32 Compilers cannot check for logical errors in a program. *True*
[Compilers can only check syntax errors (and some semantic errors)]

A33 Type checking is done during syntax analysis. *False*
[Type checking is done during semantic analysis phase]

A34 Interpreted languages support Dynamic Typing. *True*

A35 Interpreters do not generate any intermediate code. *True*

A36 Symbol tables are also used during interactive debugging. ***True***

A37 In an interpreter, lexical analysis, parsing and type-checking are done just as in a compiler. ***True***

A38 In an interpreter, code is generated from the syntax tree. ***False***

A39 In an interpreter, the syntax tree is processed directly to evaluate expressions and execute statements. ***True***

A40 An interpreter may process the same portion of the syntax tree (ex. body of a loop) many times. ***True***

A41 Interpretation is typically slower than executing a compiled program. ***True***

A42 Developing an interpreter is usually simpler than developing a compiler. ***True***

A43 Compilation and interpretation may be not be combined to implement a programming language. ***False***
[They can be combined – the compiler would translate the source code to an intermediate code (similar to assembly code), which is then interpreted and executed]

A44 Interpreter are better suited than compilers during program development. ***True***

A45 An interpreter works on a representation that is closer to the source code than is compiled code. ***True***

A46 The error messages can be more precise and informative (in general) in a compiler than in an interpreter. ***False***

A47 Compilers can detect runtime errors. ***False***

A48 Compilers cannot detect logical errors. ***True***

IOIOIOIOIOIOIOIOIOIOIOIOIOIOIOIOIOIOIOIOIOIOIOIOIOIOIOIOI

Fill-in the-blanks Questions

A1 The software which translates high-level language program into machine language program is known as ***compiler***.

A2   The software which manages various resources and activities in a computer is known as the ***operating system***.

A3   A(n) ***Integrated Development Environment (IDE)*** provides facilities such as editing, compiling, running, and debugging during program development.

A4   A program which compiles without error(s) but terminates abnormally when run is said to have ***runtime*** error.

A5   A program which compiles without error(s) but produces incorrect result(s) is said to have ***logic*** (***logical***) error.

A6   ***Algol-60*** strongly influenced the design of numerous imperative languages.

A7   The language used to describe another language is known as ***metalanguage***.

A8   ***Linker*** combines a number of independently compiled programs into an executable file.

A9   Languages in which a program specifies *how* a computation is to be done (*i.e.*, the steps of computation) are called ***imperative*** languages.

A10   Languages in which a program specifies *what* computation is to be done (without details of the steps) are called ***declarative*** languages.

A11   A programming languages that supports more than one programming paradigm is known as ***multi-paradigm*** language.

A12   **C** was developed as a systems programming language for the development of UNIX.

A13   If each feature of a language can be used in conjunction with all other features, the features are said to be ***orthogonal***.

A14   What a program looks like (or its structure) is called its ***syntax***.

A15   The execution or meaning of each feature in a language is called its ***semantics***.

A16   Statement-oriented languages are also called ***procedural*** languages.

A17 The system program which combines separately compiled segments of a program into one executable is called a ***linker***.

A18 The process of replacing symbolic references or names of libraries with actual usable addresses in memory before running a program, is known as ***relocation***.

A19 Relocation is done at compile time by the ***linker***.

A20 Relocation is done at runtime by the ***relocating loader***.

A21 The ***loader*** puts together all of the executable object files into memory for execution.

A22 The ***preprocessor*** is a program that works on the source code before the compilation.

A23 The macros in a program is expanded by the ***preprocessor***.

A24 A program written in a high-level language is known as ***source program*** (or ***source code***).

A25 The result of compiling a program is known as ***object code***.

A26 The result of combining several objects files into what the machine can execute is known as ***executable image***.

A27 The rule or pattern specifying how a certain input sequence should be mapped to an output sequence according to a defined procedure is known as a ***macro***.

A28 The reference to a function in a file, which has been defined in a different file, will be resolved at ***link*** time.

A29 Sections of code that have to be included in many places in a program with little or no changes is known as ***boilerplate*** code.

A30 The most commonly used representation inside the computer is known as ***two's complement***.

A31 Unlike float or double data type, the ***decimal*** data type can store the exact decimal value (within the allowable range).

A32 Languages where type checking happens at run time are known as ***dynamically*** typed languages.

A33 Languages that allow blocks to be nested are said to have ***block structure***.

A34 Separation of logical view of data from its underlying implementation is known as ***data*** abstraction.

A35 Separation of logical view of action from its underlying implementation is known as ***procedural*** abstraction.

A36 A program which does not compile is said to have ***syntax*** error(s).

A37 A program which compiles without error(s) but terminates abnormally when run is said to have ***runtime*** error.

A38 Separately compiled files of a program are combined into one executable by the ***linker***.

A39 External references are resolved at run time by a ***dynamic*** linker.

A40 The intermediate code generated from the source code by Java compiler is known as ***Java bytecode***.

A41 The software that interprets (or compiles) Java bytecode is known as ***Java virtual machine (JVM)***.

A42 The data type which is not defined in terms of other types is known as ***primitive type***.
[The most common primitive types are characters, integers, floating point numbers, Boolean values.]

A43 The accuracy of the fractional part of a floating point (real) number is known as ***precision***.

A44 Just-in-time (JIT) compilation translates ***intermediate*** code to ***(executable) machine*** code.

A45 In most programming languages the two types of floating-point numbers supported are `float` and `double`.

A46 The database of a PROLOG program consists of ***facts*** and ***rules***.

A47 In the ***declarative*** category of languages, 'what' needs to be computed is specified, and 'how' it is carried out is left to the system.

A48 The primary platform on which *C#* is used is the *.NET framework*.

IOIOIOIOIOIOIOIOIOIOIOIOIOIOIOIOIOIOIOIOIOIOIOIOIOIOIOI

Essay-type Questions

A1 List the major programming language paradigms.
1. Procedural (Imperative)
2. Functional
3. Declarative
4. Object–Oriented
5. Scripting

A2 What is aliasing?

Aliasing refers to two different variables having access to (bound to) the same memory location(s).

A3 Which is the most prevalent computer architecture, and what category of programming languages have been designed around them?
The von Neumann architecture is the most prevalent architecture and the imperative languages have been designed around them.

A4 Under what condition(s) is the compilation efficiency is preferred to the optimality of the object code produced?
For students (learning environments) and in rapid prototyping environments where a program is repeatedly compiled and the program executed, the speed of compilation is more important than the optimality of the object code.

A5 What is Just-in-time (JIT) compilation?
A JIT system initially translates programs into an intermediary language. Then, during execution, it compiles the intermediary language methods into machine code when they are called.

A6 What role does the symbol table play in a compiler?
The symbol table (generated by the lexical and syntax analyzers) contains the type and attribute information of each of the user defined names in the program, and serves as a database in the compilation process.

A7 What does a linker do?

The linker puts together (combines) the object code of the program produced by the compiler and the object codes of user/system libraries into the executable code.

A8 What is the von Neumann bottleneck?

The computation takes place in a von Neumann architecture computer by the CPU fetching instructions and data from the memory, operating on the data, and storing the results in memory. The connection between the CPU and memory is a limiting factor in the speed of computation and is called the von Neumann bottleneck, since the CPU execution is much faster than the memory access.

A9 What is a nonprocedural language?

A nonprocedural language is one where the actual sequence of computations is not laid out specifying how the computation should be carried out.

A10   What was the first application for Java?

Java was developed with the software for embedded consumer electronics systems in mind. However, it became extremely popular for Web programming and in graphical browsers.

A11 For what application area is JavaScript most widely used?

It is used as embedded code in HTML documents to create dynamic HTML documents.

A12   What does an XSLT processor do?

XSLT (eXensible Stylesheet Language Transformations) processor is a program which takes an XML data document and an XSLT document and transforms the XML data document into another XML document using the transformations described in the XSLT document.

A13   What does a JSP (Java Server Pages) processor do?

A JSP processor residing on a Web server system converts a JSP document (which a mixture of HTML and Java) into a servlet when it is requested by a browser.

A14   List the different language processers that a typical integrated software development environment would have.

A typical integrated software development environment includes many different kinds of language processors such as assemblers, interpreters, compilers, linkers, loaders, debuggers, and profilers.

A15   Give examples of syntax errors (in C, C++, Java, and similar languages).
a) Not having a closing quotation mark on a string.
b) Not having a semicolon at the end of a statement
c) Use of misspelt reserved words (ex. 'brake' in place of 'break')
d) Using reserved words with capitalization (ex. "While" in place of "while")
e) Not having a corresponding closing brace (}) for an opening brace ({)
f) Putting spaces between some relational operators ("!=", "<=", ">=", "==")
g) Using the modulus operator, %, with non-integer operands.
h) Not having a return statement in a method that is defined to return a value.

A16   Give examples of run-time errors (in C, C++, Java, and similar languages).
a) Division by 0.
b) Termination due to excessive memory use (Memory leak).
c) Caught in an infinite loop

A17   Give examples of logical errors (in C, C++, Java, and similar languages).
a) Use of '=' where an equality check ('==') is intended.
b) Having an 'else' for an unintended 'if'.
c) Using "<=" in place of ">=" (and vice versa)
d) Mixing variables of different types (ex. integer and double types) in expressions without explicit cast.
e) Omitting the **break** clause from **switch** statements.

IOIOIOIOIOIOIOIOIOIOIOIOIOIOIOIOIOIOIOIOIOIOIOIOIOIOIOIOI

B. Names, Bindings, and Scopes

True/False Questions

B1 JavaScript does not support dynamic binding. *False*
[As an example, a variable can be assigned any value at any time during execution. A variable can be assigned an integer value at some instant, and may be assigned a string at another instant]

B2 The lifetime of static variables is the entire program execution time. *True*

B3 The binding of a variable can change during the course of program under dynamic binding. *True*

B4 The global variables are allocated on stack. *False*
[Global variables are allocated in an area of memory called data area]

B5 Stack dynamic variables are bound to memory locations at compile time. *False*
[Stack dynamic variables come into existence when execution reaches the statement where they are declared or used as arguments in function calls]

B6 In some languages, the type of a variable could change during the program execution. *True*
[Yes, in languages using dynamic binding]

B7 A static variable is allocated in the stack area of memory. *False*
[Static variables are allocated in the data area of memory]

B8 An explicit heap dynamic variable needs a function or operator for its creation. *True*
[An operator (ex. new) or a constructor method is used to create an explicit heap dynamic variable]

B9 The global variables in a program are *always* visible inside all subprograms. *False*
[A local variable declared within a block with the same name and type as a global variable will hide the global variable inside that block]

B10 Dynamic binding can occur before the start of execution of the program. *False*

[Information about the storage location and data type in case of dynamic binding, is not available at compile time]

B11 Dynamic allocation of memory is done by the compiler. *False*
[The dynamic allocation of memory is done by the run-time system]

B12 A memory location could have multiple variable names referring to it. *True*
[This is known as aliasing. It is possible and valid]

B13 A variable name cannot refer to multiple memory locations at the same time. *True*
[Note that multiple names can refer to the same memory location, while a name cannot refer to multiple locations]

B14 The lifetime of a stack–dynamic variable is the entire execution time of the program. *False*
[Stack dynamic variable comes into existence when execution reaches the statement in the block where it is declared or when a function is called and ceases to exist when execution of the block finishes or the function returns]

B15 Static variables are never allocated on stack. *True*
[Stack area of memory is used for allocation of stack-dynamic variables. Static variables are allocated in the data area of memory. Note that 'data', 'stack', and 'heap' are logical areas of memory for the allocation and management of different kinds of variables]

B16 Dynamically allocated memory is always allocated in the stack area of memory. *False*
[A category of dynamically allocated memory is allocated in the 'heap' area of memory]

B17 Dynamic scoping is based on the calling sequence of subprograms. *True*

B18 A heap–dynamic variable must be explicitly deallocated in C++. *True*

B19 In all languages, the scope of variables can be solely determined by the program text. *False*
[In dynamic scoping, the scope of variables cannot be determined by the program text, but on the calling sequences]

B20 Multiple variables of the same name but with different scopes can be used in the same program in C++. *True*

B21 During run-time, an arbitrary number of memory cells need to be allocated for the parameters and local variables to support recursion. **_True_**
[The 'depth' of recursion is known only at run-time, and the amount of memory required may not be known *a priori*]

B22 In most programming languages, the global variables are initialized. **_True_**

B23 In most programming languages, the local variables are initialized. **_False_**

B24 Using global variables instead of parameter passing increases execution speed. **_True_**
[Use of global variables is faster, since it does not have the overhead of allocation / deallocation of variables on stack required in the case of parameter passing]

B25 In a static array, the subscript ranges are not known before run time. **_False_**
[The array subscript range for a static array must be specified at compile time]

B26 In static binding, a variable can only be assigned values of the type specified at the time its declaration. **_True_**

B27 In dynamic binding, a variable can only be assigned a value of a particular type during the execution of the program. **_False_**

B28 The memory allocated to every variable is guaranteed to be at the same address for the entire duration of program execution. **_False_**
[In dynamic binding, a name can refer to different variables and memory locations at different points in the program execution]

B29 There could be cases where the declaration of a variable may not necessarily allocate the memory for it at compile time. **_True_**
[Declaration of local variables in functions will not be allocated memory at compile time. For those variables, the memory would be allocated when execution reaches their declaration statement]

B30 Creation of dynamic data structures and objects cannot be done in static allocation. **_True_**

B31 Static allocation would not work for recursive routines. **_True_**

[The recursion depth is usually never known until the function is called. It depends on the value(s) of the argument(s)]

B32 All global variables are static variables. *__True__*

B33 All static variables are global variables. *__False__*
[Local variables in subprograms can be declared to be static]

B34 Languages with dynamic binding are usually interpreted (than compiled). *__True__*

B35 Local variables do not have default values. *__True__*

B36 Local variables are initialized with default values when they are declared. *__False__*

B37 It is possible for the type of a variable to be statically bound and it's storage to be dynamically bound. *__True__*
[This is the case for stack-dynamic variables]

B38 The type of a stack dynamic variable is not statically bound. *__False__*

B39 The types of stack dynamic variables can change during execution. *__False__*

B40 The type of an explicit heap dynamic variable is statically bound. *__True__*
[An explicit heap-dynamic variable must have a type at declaration which stays unchanged throughout the lifetime of the variable. It may, however, be bound to different memory locations during its lifetime]

B41 The type of an implicit heap dynamic variable is statically bound. *__False__*
[An implicit heap-dynamic variable can be assigned different values corresponding to different data types at different instances during execution]

B42 Static scoping is less efficient than dynamic scoping. *__False__*

B43 The readability of code using static scoping is better than that using dynamic scoping. *__True__*

[The scope and visibility of variables under static scoping may easily be determined by the text of the source file (which is spatial), rather than in dynamic scoping which depends on the calling sequences (which is temporal)]

B44   When a subprogram / method finishes and returns to the caller, all of the associated stack-dynamic variables are implicitly deallocated. ***True***

B45   Operators or methods are required for the allocation of stack–dynamic variables. ***False***

B46   Operators or methods are required for the allocation of explicit–heap dynamic variables. ***True***

B47   Operators or methods are required for the allocation of implicit–heap dynamic variables. ***False***

B48   Garbage collection is be used in the case of explicit heap–dynamic variables. ***False***
[Garbage collection is used for implicit heap–dynamic variables]

B49   There will be memory leaks in the use of static variables. ***False***

B50   There will be memory leaks with stack-dynamic variables. ***False***
[Stack-dynamic variables are automatically deallocated after the exit of the block where those variables are declared]

B51   There will not be memory leaks with explicit heap dynamic variables. ***False***
[There could be memory leaks in the case of explicit heap dynamic variables if the corresponding 'delete' is missing for an already allocated memory before the pointer (or reference) to memory is being assigned to another new allocation]

B52   There will not be memory leaks with implicit heap dynamic variables. ***True***
[In case of implicit heap dynamic variables, garbage collection will periodically reclaim unreferenced heap memory]

B53   Under dynamic scoping, the scope can be determined at compile time. ***False***

[In dynamic scoping, the scope of variables depends on the calling sequence, and can be determined only at run-time]

B54 The type of an implicit heap-dynamic variable can change during runtime. *__True__*

B55 The type of an explicit heap-dynamic variable can change during runtime. *__False__*

B56 The type of a stack-dynamic variable can change during runtime. *__False__*

B57 Dynamically allocated memory can sometimes have a lifetime equal to the entire program execution time. *__True__*

B58 Memory leak is not a problem in languages using implicit deallocation. *__False__*
[Languages using implicit deallocation depend on garbage collection to reclaim allocated, but unreferenced memory. However, garbage collection may not be 'perfect', which leads to memory leak]

B59 There is no difference between shallow copy and deep copy in the case of primitive data types. *__True__*

B60 In a dynamically typed language, all type checking is done at runtime. *__True__*

B61 Most dynamically typed languages are interpreted. *__True__*

B62 In C++, a variable can be defined anywhere in the program where a statement can appear. *__True__*

B63 In C++, namespaces cannot be nested within another. *__False__*

B64 C++ supports dynamic binding of named constants to values. *__True__*

B65 Java objects are explicit heap dynamic. *__True__*

B66 Java provides no explicit operator or method to delete explicit heap dynamic variables. *__True__*

B67 Java does not support dynamic binding of named constants to values. *__False__*

B68   In Java, the packages are not hierarchical. **_True_**

B69   In Java, there are no standalone subprograms. **_True_**

IOIOIOIOIOIOIOIOIOIOIOIOIOIOIOIOIOIOIOIOIOIOIOIOIOI

Fill-in the-blanks Questions

B1   The **_scope_** of a variable is the segment of the program within which it is declared and used.

B2   The region of the program in which a variable is declared and can be referred to (used) is called its **_scope_**.

B3   During a program's execution, the interval in which memory is assigned to a variable is known as the **_lifetime_** of the variable.

B4   Under **_static_** or **_lexical_** scope, the visibility of variables can be determined based solely on the program text.

B5   It is possible to determine the scope of a variable by looking only at the program text in language using **_static_** or **_lexical_** scope.

B6   The listing of variable names and their types in a program is referred to as **_explicit_** declaration.

B7   The time during which a variable is bound to a specific memory location is called its **_lifetime_**.

B8   A variable that is bound to a value once, and does not change thereafter, is known as **_named constant_**.

B9   A **_static_** binding occurs before run time and remains unchanged throughout program execution.

B10   The block (range of statements) in which a variable is visible, is referred to as its **_scope_**.

B11   The collection of all variables that are visible in a statement is known as its **_referencing environment_**.

B12 The set of bindings in effect at a given point in a program is known as *referencing environment*.

B13 The (common) term used to denote the ability to select subprograms at run-time is *late binding* or *dynamic binding*.

B14 *Binding* is an association between an entity and its attribute(s).

B15 *Static* binding occurs before runtime.

B16 Assignment statement essentially binds *name* to *value*.

B17 *Dynamic* scope is based on calling sequences of subprograms.

B18 Under *dynamic scoping*, the scope of a variable cannot be determined at compile time.

B19 *Descriptor* is the collection of the attributes of a variable.

B20 *Reserved word* is a special word in a programming language that cannot be used as a variable name.

B21 The *extern* specifier indicates that a variable is defined elsewhere.

B22 A *named constant* is a variable that is bound to a value only once.

B23 In each of the following scenarios, at what stage/time does the binding gets defined?
  i.   Operator symbols to operations: *language design time*
  ii. Floating point type to a representation: *language implementation time*
  iii. Variables to (data) types (in C, C++, Java): *compile time*
  iv. Static variables (in C, C++) to memory cells: *load time*
  v.   Non–static variables to memory cells: *run time*

B24 The *L–value* of a variable is its *address*.

B25 The *R–value* of a variable is its *value*.

B26 The six attributes of a variable are *Name*, *Address*, *Value*, *Type*, *Scope*, and *Lifetime*.

B27   A variable which is visible in a statement (program unit), but not declared within the block where the statement appears is known as *__nonlocal__* variable.

B28   The allocation of all the data objects at compile time is known as *__static__* allocation.

B29   With explicit deallocation, absence of matching deallocation for every allocation leads to *__memory leaks__*.

B30   The number and size of all possible objects is known at compile time under *__static__* allocation.

B31   A variable that is bound to a memory cell during the entire execution time of the program is known as *__static variable__*.

B32   Recursive routines require *__dynamic__* allocation.

B33   The association of an identifier in a program with a memory location (address) is called *__binding__*.

B34   The automatic detection of the data type of an expression or a variable based on the context is known as *__type inference__*.

B35   A variable getting bound to a type when it is assigned a value is known as *__dynamic__* binding.

B36   In *__dynamic__* binding, a variable can be assigned a value of any type during the execution of the program.

B37   Languages with *__static__* binding are usually compiled (than interpreted).

B38   Two distinct (logical) areas of memory where dynamic variables are allocated are *__stack__* and *__heap__*.

B39   Memory that is allocated by OS before program starts execution is known as *__static memory__*.

B40   Variables which are allocated storage at runtime when execution reaches their declaration statement are known as *__stack–dynamic__* variables.

B41 Operators or constructor methods are required for the allocation of *explicit heap–dynamic* variables.

B42 *Explicit heap–dynamic* variables are bound to storage at the time of execution of the operator / constructor methods.

B43 *Implicit heap–dynamic* variables are bound to storage at the time of assignment of a value.

B44 Garbage collection must be used in the case of *implicit heap–dynamic* variables.

B45 The arguments of subprograms / methods are of type *stack dynamic*.

B46 The types of stack dynamic variables are bound at *compile* time.

B47 The type of *implicit heap-dynamic* variable gets defined only when a value is assigned at runtime.

B48 The periodic, automatic reclamation by the system, of the dynamically allocated memory is known as *garbage collection*.

B49 A *dynamic* binding can change during the execution of a program.

B50 In a *heap-dynamic* array the binding of subscript ranges can change any number of times during the array's life time.

B51 In C++ and Java, the variables declared in methods are, by default, of type *stack dynamic*.

B52 The same name bound to multiple entities at the same time is known as *polymorphism*.

B53 Multiple names bound to the same entity at the same time is known as *aliasing*.

B54 The same use of a variable could refer to any of several different declarations of that variable at run time with *dynamic* scope.

B55 Use of a name referring to its declaration in the most recently called, but not-yet-terminated procedure is called *dynamic* scope.

B56 In C++, by default all method binding is *static*.

B57   In Java, method binding, by default, is ***dynamic***.

B58   In Java, the keyword used for method declaration to indicate that the method cannot be overridden by subclasses is, **`final`**.

B59   In Java, a class that cannot be subclassed must be declared **`final`**.

B60   In Java, if the method is declared `final`, ***static*** binding occurs.

IOIOIOIOIOIOIOIOIOIOIOIOIOIOIOIOIOIOIOIOIOIOIOIOIOIOI

Essay-type Questions

B1 List the (major) *entities* that are defined and manipulated programs of contemporary, procedural languages.
The common entities are, types, variables, constants, blocks, functions, methods, classes, modules, operators, parameters, packages, etc.

B2   In a *block–structured* language using *static scoping*, what is the rule for finding the correct declaration of the nonlocal variables?
The declaration of the nonlocal variables is searched in the increasingly larger enclosing blocks until it is found. If not found, it is an error.

B3   Briefly explain why dynamically typed languages are (usually) interpreted rather than compiled.
If the types of operands for an operator are not known at compile time, the compiler cannot generate the appropriate machine instructions. For example, the operator "+" is usually overloaded – it can have multiple meanings. With integer operands, it performs integer addition, and with string operands, it performs concatenation. For machine code generation, the exact action must be known.

B4   How is the correct declaration of nonlocal variables found under *dynamic scoping*?
It is found by going over the declarations in the calling sequences of the subprograms in reverse chronological order (most recent first).

B5   What is an example of an error in a program which could result in exhaustion of memory for the *stack–dynamic* variables?
Recursive calling of function(s) of considerable 'depth', which exhausts the stack memory.

B6   What is an example of an error in a program which could result in exhaustion of memory for the *heap–dynamic* variables?
Repeated allocation of heap memory without 'returning' / 'releasing' memory that is no longer used, back to the heap (This scenario is also called *memory leak*).

B7   Give examples of places in a program where the declared variables are *stack dynamic*.
a) Variables declared in subprograms
b) Variables passed as arguments to subprograms

B8   How are *explicit heap dynamic* variables deallocated and returned to the memory pool?
Using the 'destructive' functions or operators (such as **delete**)

B9   Briefly describe the lifetimes of static, stack dynamic, explicit heap-dynamic, and implicit heap-dynamic variables.

Variable type	Start of existence	End of existence
Static	Compile time (before the program execution starts)	Until end of program
Stack dynamic	When the declaration statement is encountered during runtime	When the block where it is declared finishes execution
Explicit heap-dynamic	When an operator or constructor method is used to create the variable	When an operator or destructor method is used to 'remove' the variable
Implicit heap-dynamic	When the variable is assigned a value	When the Garbage Collector reclaims it

IOIOIOIOIOIOIOIOIOIOIOIOIOIOIOIOIOIOIOIOIOIOIOIOIOIOIOIOIOIOI

C. Data Types

True/False Questions

C1   All integer values (within the machine representable range) can be represented without loss of precision. **_True_**

C2   All floating point values (within the machine representable range) can be represented without loss of precision. **_False_**

C3   A primitive data type can be defined in terms of other types. **_False_**

C4   The limited dynamic strings of C/C++ do not require run–time descriptors. **_True_**

C5   The values in a subrange type need not be contiguous. **_False_**

C6   In all languages, an array should be homogeneous – consisting of elements of the same type. **_False_**
[For example, Perl, Python, JavaScript, Ruby support elements to be of different types]

C7   In the record type, all elements (fields) should be of the same type. **_False_**

C8   Pointers require different memory sizes based on the data types of objects they point to. **_False_**

C9   The members of a record type may reside in locations which are not adjacent. **_False_**

C10 The elements of a heterogeneous array are always allocated consecutive memory locations. **_False_**

C11 Java does not support the pointer type. **_True_**

C12 C# supports both pointer and reference types. **_True_**

C13 The contents of a pointer is a memory address. **_True_**

C14 No arithmetic operation at all can be done on a pointer type. **_False_**
[C and C++ support pointer arithmetic operations]

C15 In every language, the array subscript has to be of integer type. **_False_**

[For example, Ada and Pascal support array subscripts to be characters]

C16 The array index is always of type integer in all languages. *False*

C17 The **int** datatype has different variations in C, C++, and Java. *True*

C18 Several languages provide **string** as a primitive data type. *True*

C19 There are some languages where the array subscript could be other than the integer type. *True*

C20 The exact value of every floating point number within the allowed range can be stored in the computer. *False*

C21 Typeless languages offer great flexibility for the programmer. *True*

C22 Type checking in a language supporting dynamic type binding can be done at compile time. *False*

C23 Type checking in languages does not necessarily reduce programmer errors. *False*

C24 C++ is a type-safe language. *False*

C25 The value of a variable of *pointer* type is any integer. *False*
[It must be a valid address within the program's address space]

C26 The value of a variable of *pointer* type is a valid address. *True*

C27 Primitive types are not reference types. *True*

C28 Array types are reference types. *True*

C29 In widening conversion, the magnitude of the converted value is not maintained. *False*

C30 Integer to floating-point (widening) conversion will never result in loss of precision. *False*
[The number of 'digits' for the mantissa part of a floating point number could be less than that of an integer]

C31 Implicit type conversions (coercions) can be specified in programming language syntax. *False*

C32 Implicit type conversions (coercions) can be specified in programming language semantics. ***True***

C33 Mixed mode expression may give incorrect results. ***True***

C34 Coercion (by itself) specified in a programming language always gives correct results in mixed-mode expressions. ***False***

C35 Implicit type conversion (coercion) provided in the language may never lead to logical errors. ***False***
[If **i** and **j** are integers with values 1 and 2 respectively, and **sum** is of type double, then **sum = i / j** will assign 0.0 to **sum**, since the '/' is done on integers, and the result is converted to double. Therefore, if the intended result is 0.5, then explicit type conversion (cast) is needed, and **sum = (double)i / j** would yield the correct result]

C36 Casting may be necessary in addition to coercion for correct results. ***True***

C37 A type mismatch always results in a runtime error. ***False***
[Use of appropriate explicit type conversion (cast), together with the implicit type conversion (coercion) provided in the language can ensure correct results]

C38 For static arrays, the array subscripts are fixed at compile time. ***True***

C39 The type of a static variable is known before runtime. ***True***

C40 The type of a static variable can change during runtime. ***False***

C41 The type of a stack dynamic variable can change during run time. ***False***

C42 The type of an explicit heap–dynamic variable can change even after the allocation of storage. ***False***

C43 The type of an implicit heap–dynamic variable can change several times during execution. ***True***
[For implicit heap–dynamic variables, the type gets determined by when the variable is assigned a value. Different types/values can be assigned at different types]

C44 Heap dynamic variables do not have an explicit name when created. ***True***

C45 In Java, there are no operators or methods for deallocation of class instances. ***True***

C46 The size of a stack-dynamic array can change during runtime, after the array has been allocated. ***False***

C47 The subscript ranges of a stack-dynamic array can change during runtime, after the array has been allocated. ***False***

C48 The subscript ranges of a stack-dynamic array may not be known at compile time. ***True***

C49 The size of a stack-dynamic array may not be known at compile time. ***True***

C50 The size of a stack-dynamic array can be specified at run-time. ***True***

C51 Coercion (implicit type conversion) is always done at run-time in statically typed languages. ***False***
[In statically typed languages, coercion (implicit type conversion) is done at compile time]

C52 Type checks are done only at compile time. ***False***
[Smalltalk, Perl, Ruby, Python have type checks done at runtime]

C53 Multidimensional arrays in C are arrays of arrays. ***True***

C54 The fields of a record are allocated consecutive memory locations. ***True***

C55 In C# class type checking can be specified to be done at run time rather than compile time. ***True***

C56 In Java, an array may contain only primitive types. ***False***
[In Java, an array may contain both primitive and object types]

IOIOIOIOIOIOIOIOIOIOIOIOIOIOIOIOIOIOIOIOIOIOIOIOIOIOIOIOIOI

Fill-in the-blanks Questions

C1 ***Boolean*** is the simplest of all data types.

C2 The type in which the range of all possible values is associated with the set of positive integers, is known as ***ordinal type***.

C3 ***Sub–range*** is ordered contiguous subsequence of an ordinal type.

C4 ***Data type*** refers to a collection of data objects and a set of predefined operations on those objects.

C5 A *jagged* array is one in which the lengths of the rows need not be the same.

C6 ***Record (Struct)*** is a possibly heterogeneous aggregate of data elements where the individual members are identified by names.

C7 A ***union*** is a type whose members may store different type values at different times.

C8 ***Type checking*** ensures that the operands of an operator are of compatible types.

C9 The application of an operator to an operand of an inappropriate type results in ***type*** error.

C10 In a ***strongly typed*** programming language most of the type (mismatch) errors are detected at compile time.

C11 A ***strongly typed*** language has stricter type checking rules at compile time,

C12 In C–based languages, explicit type conversions are called ***casts***.

C13 A language is said to be ***type-safe*** if an object cannot be used as an object of an unrelated type.

C14 ***Dereferencing*** refers to accessing the value of a variable via the pointer to the variable.

C15 The value of a variable of *pointer* type is a(n) ***address***.

C16 A ***dangling*** pointer is one that contains the address of heap–dynamic variable that has been deallocated.

C17 In ***narrowing*** conversion, the converted type cannot include all of the values of the original type.

C18 The **_widening_** conversion is usually safe (magnitude of the converted value is maintained).

C19 **_Associative array_** is an unordered collection of data elements using key–value pairs.

C20 The underlying implementation of enumeration types is done using **_integers_**.

C21 Explicit type conversion in C–based languages is called **_cast_**.

C22 Values of a(n) **_enumeration_** type are represented by default as consecutive integers starting from zero.

C23 A **_subtype_** is a restriction on an existing type.

C24 Accessing an element of an array by name (key) is done in a(n) **_associative_** array.

C25 Check for type safety done at compile time is known as **_static type checking_**.

C26 Check for type safety done at runtime is known as **_dynamic type checking_**.

C27 Type checking is done at **_compile_** time in statically typed languages.

C28 Type checking is done at runtime in **_dynamically_** typed languages.

C29 The implicit/automatic type conversion of one data type to another, done by the compiler or interpreter, is known as **_coercion_**.

C30 The explicit conversion of a datatype to another type, done by the programmer, is known as **_casting_**.

C31 Storage allocation for a static array is done at **_compile_** time.

C32 The size of a **_heap-dynamic_** array can change during runtime, after the array has been allocated.

C33 The subscript ranges of a **_heap-dynamic_** array can change during runtime, after the array has been allocated.

C34 Multidimensional arrays in C are stored in **_row-major_** order.

C35   In multi-byte storage in a word, storing the least significant byte at the lowest address, called ***little endian***.

C36   In multi-byte storage in a word, storing the least significant byte at the highest address, called ***big endian***.

C37   The data with a value that is distinct from all legal data values, which is used to detect the end of the data, is known as ***sentinel***.

C38   In a static array, the subscript ranges are [statically?/dynamically?] ***statically*** bound and storage allocation is done at ***compile*** time.

C39   In a fixed stack-dynamic array, the subscript ranges are [statically?/dynamically?] ***statically*** bound, and the allocation is done at ***run*** time.

C40   In ***fixed heap-dynamic*** arrays, the binding of subscript ranges and storage allocation is done at run time, but do not change during execution.

C41   In ***heap-dynamic*** arrays, the binding of subscript ranges and storage allocation are dynamic and can change during execution.

IOIOIOIOIOIOIOIOIOIOIOIOIOIOIOIOIOIOIOIOIOIOIOIOIOIOIOIOI

Essay-type Questions

C1   What is a data type?
A data type consists of a set of data values (or objects) and a set of predefined operations on those values (or objects). For example, the integer data type consists of all integer values representable in a computer, and all the valid operations on integer data such as $+$, $-$, $*$, $/$, $<$, $\leq$, etc.

C2   What is the *type system* of a programming language?
It consists of the set of data types and rules governing their compatibility, equivalence, and conversions.

C3   What is type checking?
Type checking is a check that ensures that the type of the value of an expression is compatible with the type of the target variable to which it will be assigned. It also checks if the type of the actual

132

parameter (argument) is compatible (matches) with that of the formal parameter in a subprogram call.

C4   What is an abstract data type (ADT)?
ADT is a model which specifies a collection of data objects and the set of operations on these objects. It only specifies the behavior of the objects and operations at a level of abstraction, and does not specify the details of the storage of the objects nor the implementation of the operations.

C5   Give the formula for computing the starting byte address of the kth element of a 1–D array whose first element starts at address P, and each element is of size S.
$$P + (k - 1) * S$$

C6   Consider a 2–D array A of N x M elements, each element of size S bytes. Assuming column-major order, by how many bytes offset will the element $A[1,2]$ be from $A[1,1]$ (the first element)?
$N * S$ bytes
In column-major order, the elements of the first column are stored contiguously, followed by the second column, and so on.

C7   Consider a 2–D array A of N x M elements, each element of size S bytes. Assuming column-major order, the first element $A[1,1]$ is at address P, what is the starting byte address of element $A[k, l]$?
$$P + (k - 1) * NS + (l - 1) * S$$

C8   Briefly describe the difference between *shallow* copy and *deep* copy.
In case of primitive data types (ex. character, integer, etc.), there is no difference. The value of a variable of a given primitive type is copied onto the other variable of the same type. In case of *shallow* copy of objects (non-primitive data), only the reference to the object is copied onto a variable which references the object. Thus there are two references which refer (point) to the same object, and no new object is created. In case of *deep* copy of objects, a new object is created as well as a reference to it. The reference to the original object as well as the values of the fields of the original object are copied onto the newly created ones.

C9   What is garbage collection?
It refers to periodic, automatic reclamation by the system of the dynamically allocated memory (specifically, it is the implicit heap-

dynamic memory) to user programs. It does so by identifying inaccessible and previously allocated but currently unused memory blocks and returning them to the 'free' memory.

C10 How is garbage collection done?
There are two broad garbage collection mechanisms. In one of them, a count of the number of pointers currently pointing to each block is maintained, and when the count goes to zero, the block is deallocated. In the other one, all accessible blocks are marked and then all unmarked (inaccessible) blocks are collected.

IOIOIOIOIOIOIOIOIOIOIOIOIOIOIOIOIOIOIOIOIOIOIOIOIOIOIOIOI

D. Expressions and Assignment Statements

True/False Questions

D1   All expressions will produce side effects. *False*

D2   Evaluation of some expressions could change the value(s) of the components in the expression. *True*

D3   Assignment statements produce side effects. *True*

D4   The statements in functional languages do not have side effects. *True*

D5   In Java, the sub-expressions are executed from left to right. *True*

D6   In C++, the sub-expressions are executed in any order. *True*

D7   In a short-circuit evaluation, the result of an expression can be determined without evaluating all of the sub-expressions. *True*

D8   Arithmetic expressions can be the operands of relational expressions. *True*

D9   Boolean expressions cannot be the operands of relational operators. *False*
[ex. `false != true` and `false == true` are valid, although the resulting values of evaluation are different]

D10 All Boolean expressions can be the operands of relational expressions. *False*
[ex. `false < true` and `false <= true` are not valid]

D11 Relational expressions can be the operands of Boolean operators. *True*
[`(5 < 7) && (4 != 3)` is valid]

D12 The result of evaluation of an arithmetic expression could be a Boolean value. *False*
[The result of evaluation of an arithmetic expression is always a numerical value]

D13 The result of evaluation of a relational expression is always a Boolean value. ***True***

D14 A completely parenthesized expression could still have ambiguities in the order of evaluation. ***False***

D15 In a short–circuit evaluation, the complete expression is *never* evaluated. ***False***

D16 Short-circuit evaluation of arithmetic expression is usually no done. ***True***

D17 Short-circuit evaluation of any expression will always give the correct results. ***False***
[If there are sub-expressions which produce side effects, then the results with short-circuit evaluation may not be correct]

D18 Control expressions must always be enclosed within parentheses. ***False***

D19 Assignments can be used as expressions in C–based languages. ***True***

D20 Assignment statements produce side effects. ***True***

D21 In most imperative programming languages, the operator precedence rules are the same. ***True***

D22 The exponentiation operator is provided by all C–family of languages. ***False***
[C, C++, C#, Java do not have built-in exponentiation operator. The operation is supported via library function]

D23 Programming language designer decides the operator precedence rules. ***True***

D24 Java guarantees left–to–right evaluation of operands. ***True***

D25 In widening conversion, the converted type can include all of the values of the original type. ***False***
[The number of 'digits' for the mantissa part of a floating point number could be less than that of an integer]

D26 Widening conversions could result in loss of precision. ***True***

D27 The choice of full evaluation or short-circuit evaluation is usually specified in the programming language. ***False***

D28 The operators and subprograms which are overloaded may not operate on entirely distinct types. ***False***

D29 In the C++ statement `cout << num`, the function is `cout`. ***False***

D30 In C++, all of the operators can be overloaded. ***False***
[For example, the class/structure member operator (.) and scope resolution operator (::) cannot be overloaded]

D31 What are the values of the following expressions?

```
int a = 2, b = 3, c = 5;
```

   vi. `a > b || c > b`   ***True***

   vii. `b < a + 2 && c <= a + b`   ***True***

   viii. `(b > c - a) || (a < c / b + 1)` ***False***

   ix. `b == b % c || a + b > c`   ***True***

   x. `(b <= c) && (b + c % a == 0)`   ***False***

IOIOIOIOIOIOIOIOIOIOIOIOIOIOIOIOIOIOIOIOIOIOIOIOIOIOIOI

Fill-in the-blanks Questions

D1 Expressions containing operators having operands of different types are known as ***mixed–mode*** expressions.

D2 ***Precedence*** and ***Associativity*** rules govern the operator evaluation order in expressions.

D3 A ***relational*** operator compares the values of its two operands.

D4 Determining the result of an expression without evaluating all of the parts of the expression is called ***short–circuit evaluation***.

D5 Operators appearing between the two of their operands are called ***infix*** operators.

D6 The normal precedence and associativity of operators can be overridden by using ***parentheses***.

D7 Computing the value of an expression without actually evaluating all components of the expression is known as ***short–circuit evaluation***.

D8 The choice of full evaluation or short-circuit evaluation is usually left to the ***compiler***.

D9 An operator having three operands is known as ***ternary*** operator.

D10 In the C++ statement **cout << num**, the function is <u>**<<**</u>.

D11 ***Overloading*** refers to multiple uses of an operator (based on different operand types).

D12 The same operator having different underlying operations based on the types of the operands at that time is known as ***operator overloading***.

IOIOIOIOIOIOIOIOIOIOIOIOIOIOIOIOIOIOIOIOIOIOIOIOIOIOI

Essay-type Questions

D1 In most programming languages, what do arithmetic expressions consist of?
  Operators, operands, parentheses, and function calls.

D2 Give examples of two operators that are not associative.
  Subtraction (–) and division (/) are not associative.
    $9 - 3 - 1$: when left associative would be $(9 - 3) - 1 = 5$;
    when right associative would be $9 - (3 - 1) = 7$
    $8 / 4 / 2$: when left associative would be $(8 / 4) / 2 = 1$
    when right associative would be $8 / (4 / 2) = 4$

D3 What are the values of **a** and **n** after the execution of the following statements?
    a = 2; n = a++; a = n++; n = a++;

    n = a++; ➔ **n** is assigned 2, and **a** is then incremented to 3, since it is post-increment.

`a = n++;` ➔ **a** is assigned 2, and **n** is then incremented to 3, since it is post-increment.
`n = a++;` ➔ **n** is assigned 2, and **a** is then incremented to 3, since it is post-increment.
Therefore, the values are: **a = 3** and **n = 2**

D4   What are the values of **a** and **n** after the execution of the following statements?
`a = 2; n = a++; a = ++n; n = a++;`

`n = a++;` ➔ **n** is assigned 2, and **a** is then incremented to 3, since it is post-increment.
`a = ++n;` ➔ **n** is incremented to 3, since it is pre-increment, and then **a** is assigned 3.
`n = a++;` ➔ **n** is assigned 3, and **a** is then incremented to 4, since it is post-increment.
Therefore, the values are: **a = 4** and **n = 3**

D5   What are the values of **a** and **n** after the execution of the following statements?
`a = 2; n = ++a; a = n++; n = ++a;`

`n = ++a;` ➔ **a** is incremented to 3, since it is pre-increment, and then **n** is assigned 3.
`a = n++;` ➔ **a** is assigned 3, and **n** is then incremented to 4, since it is post-increment.
`n = ++a;` ➔ **a** is incremented to 4, since it is pre-increment, and then **n** is assigned 4.
Therefore, the values are: **a = 4** and **n = 4**

D6   What are the values of **a** and **n** after the execution of the following statements?
`a = 2; n = ++a; a = ++n; n = ++a;`

`n = ++a;` ➔ **a** is incremented to 3, since it is pre-increment, and then **n** is assigned 3.
`a = ++n;` ➔ **n** is incremented to 4, since it is pre-increment, and then **a** is assigned 4.
`n = ++a;` ➔ **a** is incremented to 5, since it is pre-increment, and then **n** is assigned 5.
Therefore, the values are: **a = 5** and **n = 5**

D7   What is the difference between coercion and cast?
Coercion is implicit type conversion which is automatically done by the compiler. Cast is explicit type conversion done by the programmer.

D8   What is an overloaded operator?
An overloaded operator has the same form, but has different actions based on the data types. For example, the '+' (addition) operator has totally different underlying operations when the operands are integers, floating-point numbers, strings, or matrices.

D9   What is short-circuit evaluation?
In the case of compound expressions made up of sub-expressions, the value of the expression may be determined without evaluation all of the component sub-expressions, based on rules of Logic. This is known as short-circuit evaluation.

IOIOIOIOIOIOIOIOIOIOIOIOIOIOIOIOIOIOIOIOIOIOIOIOIOIOI

E. Statement-Level Control Structures

True/False Questions

E1 The **for** statement in C / C++ can be rewritten as a **while** loop. *True*

E2 The **for**, **while**, and **do-while** loops do not have equivalent expressive power. *False*

E3 Any of the **for**, **while**, and **do-while** loops can be transformed to the other having the same effect. *True*

E4 The **do-while** loop always executes at least once. *True*

E5 The **while** loop always executes at least once. *False*

E6 The **for** loop always executes at least once. *False*

E7 Multiple entries in a control structure is seldom used in practice. *True*

E8 Multiple exits in a control structure is seldom used in practice. *False*

E9 A *multiple selection control* cannot be simulated merely using multiple **if-else** statements. *False*

E10 In a *pre-test loop*, the loop body is executed at least once. *False*

E11 Theoretically, the **if** and **goto** statements are sufficient to express any needed control structure. *True*

E12 The **break** statement inside an inner loop of a nested loop will pass control out of the all the nested loops to the statement outside of the outermost loop. *False*
[The **break** statement passes control to the first statement outside of the (innermost) loop where it is executed]

E13 The **break** statement inside a loop of a nested loop will pass control out of that loop and all of its inner loops. *True*

E14 C–based languages do not provide multiple exits from control structures. *False*

E15 Assignment statements always produce side effects. *True*

E16 The *iterator* is essentially a function applied to the elements of a structured type. *True*

E17 All the three expressions of the 'for' statement in C-style languages are optional. *True*

E18 The `exp1` in `for (exp1; exp2; exp3)` can be executed more than once. *False*

E19 The `exp1` in `for (exp1; exp2; exp3)` cannot consist of multiple statements. *False*
[Multiple statements separated by commas is valid]

E20 The `exp3` in `for (exp1; exp2; exp3)` can consist of multiple statements. *True*
[Multiple statements separated by commas is valid]

E21 The `continue` control statement transfers control to the the outermost loop. *False*

E22 The `continue` control statement transfers control to the start of the loop, ignoring further statements after the `continue`. *True*

IOIOIOIOIOIOIOIOIOIOIOIOIOIOIOIOIOIOIOIOIOIOIOIOIOIOIOIOIOI

Fill-in the-blanks Questions

E1 Statement that is used to modify the order of execution is known as *control* statement.

E2 A loop whose number of iterations is determined by the numeric value of a variable is known as *counter-controlled* loop.

E3 A loop whose number of iterations is determined by the Boolean condition of an expression is known as *condition-controlled* loop.

E4   In a ***post-test*** (***do-while***) loop control structure, the loop body is executed at least once.

E5   It is more natural to use the **for** loop when the number of iterations is known *a priori* (before hand).

E6   The **break** control statement transfers control out of the smallest enclosing loop.

E7   The statement block in a ***post–test*** (or ***do–while***) control structure is executed at least once.

E8   The **break** control statement transfers control out of the smallest enclosing loop.

E9   The ***multiple–selection* (ex. switch-case)** construct allows the selection of one of a number of statements or statement groups.

E10   ***Pre–test loop* (ex. *while loop*)** causes a (compound) statement to be executed zero or more times.

E11   The **continue** control statement transfers control to the control mechanism of the smallest enclosing loop.

E12   Theoretically, the only two control statements which can achieve the effect of any control flow in a program are the **if** and **goto** statements.

E13   A control statement together with its associated block of statements is known as ***control structure***.

E14   An optional **else** clause in an **if–then** [**–else**] statement resulting in nested conditionals being ambiguous is known as ***dangling-else*** problem.

E15   The condition that must be true before execution of a statement is called ***pre-condition***.

E16   The condition that holds true after the execution of a statement is called ***post-condition***.

IOIOIOIOIOIOIOIOIOIOIOIOIOIOIOIOIOIOIOIOIOIOIOIOIOIOIOIOIOIOIOI

Essay-type Questions

E1 Do the **while**, **do-while**, and **for** loops have different
expressive powers?
The above three forms have equivalent powers in the sense that any
loop type can be transformed to any of the other loop types, while
achieving the same effect.

E2 What is the difference between **break** and **continue** statements
(of C-family) of languages?
When a **break** statement is encountered, it transfers control out of
the innermost loop to the statement right after the end of that loop.
The net effect is the termination of the innermost loop immediately
when the **break** is seen. When a **continue** statement is
encountered, the control stays within the loop, but the remainder of
the statements after the **continue** statement are skipped. The net
effect is starting the next loop iteration immediately.

E3 What are the two broad categories of control statements?
Control statements facilitate the altering of the sequential order of
statement executions. The two broad categories are, (a) conditional
selections (two–way or multi–way) and (b) loops.

E4 Briefly describe the two categories of loops.
The two loop categories are:
1. Counter–controlled loops, where the number of iterations is
determined by a counter, a variable keeping a count.
2. Logically–controlled loops, where the number of iterations is
determined by a condition which is specified by a Boolean
expression.

E5 When is it beneficial have the **if** and multiple **else if** statements
in a certain order?
Suppose the code segment has the following structure (where
statement represents a block):

```
if (cond1)
    statement1
else if (cond2)
    statement2
else if (cond3)
    statement3
    : : : : :
else
```

statementN

Suppose the average number of times each of the conditions if true is known. Then, it is beneficial to order the statements in decreasing order of the probabilities of the conditions being true. For example, if Probability (cond1) > Probability (cond2) > Probability (cond3) > ..., then using this order, the average number of condition checks is minimized. **cond1** is true most number of times on average, and the further **else if** statements will not be done, and so on.

IOIOIOIOIOIOIOIOIOIOIOIOIOIOIOIOIOIOIOIOIOIOIOIOIOIOIOIOI

F. Subprograms

True/False Questions

F1   Functions in most imperative languages can have either pass-by-value or pass-by-reference parameters. ***True***

F2   C allows return of arrays from functions. ***False***

F3   C allows return of functions from functions. ***False***

F4   Java and C# do not have functions. ***True***
[Methods are used to perform computations on objects]

F5   Global variables can never be passed as arguments to functions. ***False***
[Global variables can be passed as arguments in C-family of languages. Since it is pass-by-value, the values of global variables are copied to the parameter placeholders]

F6   In *pass-by-value*, it is possible for the called subprogram to change the values of the actual parameters of the calling subprogram. ***False***
[In pass-by-value, copies of the values of the actual arguments are used in the subprogram, and the actual values of the actual parameters (arguments) are unchanged]

F7   In the *out mode* (*pass by result*), the actual parameter is copied onto the formal parameter. ***False***
[In out mode (pass by result), the reference (pointer) to the actual parameter is copied onto the formal parameter]

F8   A function can be defined in a file, but called in another function in a different file. ***True***
[Such functions are called external functions, and the references are resolved by the linker]

F9   It is possible to define multiple functions of the same name (in a file). ***False***

F10   In a recursive call of a subprogram, there are multiple instances of its activation record. ***True***

F11   The return address of a subprogram may not always be part of its activation record. ***False***

[The return address of a subprogram must be part of its activation record, since via this the control transfers to the proper statement after the subprogram returns]

F12 Languages without stack dynamic variables cannot support recursion. *True*

F13 No local variable declared inside a program can retain its value across multiple invocations. *False*
[Local variables declared with `static` keyword retain values across multiple invocations]

F14 The static local variables of a subprogram are allocated on the stack (area of memory). *False*
[The static local variables are allocated in the data area where global variables are allocated]

F15 The static local variables of a subprogram are not allocated/deallocated upon a function entry/exit. *True*

F16 Static local variables of subprograms cannot support recursion. *True*

F17 C++ makes use of C's linkers. *True*

F18 Not all subclasses are subtypes. *True*

F19 Not all subtypes are subclasses. *True*

F20 Multidimensional arrays can never be passed as arguments. *False*
[It is possible to pass multidimensional arrays as arguments, although in an indirect way]

F21 It is not possible in any language to decide the subprogram to be called at runtime.
[It is possible in languages where subprograms can be passed as arguments, and also in C, C++ which allow pointers to functions to passed as arguments]

F22 In C++ the parameter passing for arrays is call-by-value. *False*
[In all imperative languages, arrays are always passed-by-reference, since the copying arrays are rather expensive]

F23 In pass-by-value, it is possible for the called subprogram to change the values of the actual parameters of the calling subprogram. *False*
[In pass-by-value, only copies of values of actual parameters (arguments) are used within the called subprogram, and the actual values are unchanged]

F24 A function can return multiple results back to the calling subprogram. *False*
[The syntax of functions do not allow multiple return values in most languages. However, multiple values can be returned somewhat indirectly by passing references to return values to the subprogram]

F25 Some languages support passing subprograms as arguments to other subprograms. *True*

F26 Subprogram exemplifies data abstraction. *False*
[Subprogram exemplifies process abstraction; Classes provide data abstraction]

F27 Aliasing can happen when parameters are passed by value. *False*
[Aliasing cannot happen in pass-by-value since only copies of the values of actual parameters are used. Aliasing can happen in pass-by-reference]

F28 In C / C++, a function definition can have further nested function definitions. *False*

F29 In the *out mode* (*pass by result*), the actual parameter is copied onto the formal parameter. *False*

F30 In C / C++, the local variables of functions are always stack dynamic variables. *False*
[Local variables declared with the keyword `static` are not stack dynamic]

F31 In C / C++, the local variables of functions are always stack dynamic variables, *by default*. *True*

F32 In C / C++, the lifetimes of local variables declared with `static` keyword extend beyond the time the function is active. *True*

F33 In a recursive call of a subprogram, there are multiple instances of its activation record. *True*

F34 C / C++ support both functions and procedures. *False*
[All subprograms are functions. A procedure without a return value is defined as a function returning a 'void' type]

F35 In C / C++, a function defined in a file cannot be called in another function in a different file. *False*

F36 In C/C++ functions can be passed as parameters. *False*

[C/C++ allow only pointers to functions to be passed as parameters]

F37   In C/C++ pointers to functions can be passed as parameters. ***True***

F38   The generic parameters of Java cannot be primitive types. ***True***

F39   Most imperative languages do not support returning arrays from functions. ***True***

F40   The exact type of operation in the case of overloaded operators in statically typed language may not always be determined at compile time. ***False***
[In statically typed languages, the types of the operands are known at compile time, and hence the meaning of their operator is known as well]

F41   Different versions of overloaded subprograms could have the same protocol. ***False***
[The overloaded subprograms must differ in some aspect, otherwise there will be name conflict]

F42   In generic subprograms, the types of the formal parameters are bound to types of the actual parameters at compile time. ***False***
[The types of the formal parameters of generic subprograms are bound to the actual parameters at runtime]

F43   The actions required for setting up a subprogram's call is less complicated than those of the subprogram's return. ***False***

F44   Allocation of memory for stack-dynamic variables requires explicit statements other than declarations. ***False***
[The compiler generates code for the allocation / deallocation of stack-dynamic variables; nothing more is required in the program]

F45   The format of the activation record (in most languages) is known at compile time. ***True***

F46   Subprogram parameters must always be passed via the stack. ***False***
[Although parameters are commonly passed via stack, in many RISC machines, parameters are passed via registers]

IOIOIOIOIOIOIOIOIOIOIOIOIOIOIOIOIOIOIOIOIOIOIOIOIOIOIOIOI

Fill-in the-blanks Questions

F1   The ***extern*** specifier indicates that a variable is defined elsewhere.

F2   Any two expressions in a program with the same value which can be substituted for one another, without affecting the program's behavior is known as ***referential transparency***.

F3   Referential transparency is provided by programs in (***pure***) ***functional*** languages.

F4   The number, type, order of parameters and the return type of a subprogram is collectively known as its ***protocol***.

F5   In the *in mode* (*pass by value*) the ***actual parameter*** is copied into ***formal parameter***.

F6   Parameter passing mechanism used for basic types (ex. integers, real, character) is ***pass-by-value***.

F7   In ***pass-by-value*** parameter passing, the value of the actual parameter is copied to the parameters of the called subprogram.

F8   Parameter passing mechanism used for types other than the basic types is ***pass-by-reference***.

F9   In ***pass-by- reference*** parameter passing, a pointer (or reference) to the object is passed to the called subprogram.

F10 The local variables in functions declared with the ***static*** keyword retain their values across function invocations.

F11 Operator precedence and associativity could be overridden by the use of ***parentheses***.

F12 The parameter passing mechanism used for arrays is ***pass by reference***.

F13 Ambiguities about the corresponding **if** for an **else** in a nested **if-else** structures is called the ***dangling*** **else** problem.

F14 Data abstraction is routinely used in ***object–oriented*** (kind) of languages.

F15 The return type of C# event handler is _**void**_.

F16 The types of the parameters of a C# event handler are **object** and **EventArgs**.

F17 A function definition that is not bound to an identifier is known as _**anonymous function**_.

F18 Anonymous functions are most commonly supported in _**functional**_ (category) languages.

F19 A subprogram which takes parameters of different types on different activations is known as a _**polymorphic**_ subprogram.

F20 Subprograms that do not require types of parameters to be specified, and can handle different types specified at runtime, are known as _**generic**_ subprograms.

F21 A _**generic**_ subprogram is one whose computation can be done on data of different types in different calls.

F22 In _**generic**_ subprograms, the types of the formal parameters are bound to types of the actual parameters at run time.

F23 The segment of the stack associated with each function call is called the _**activation record**_.

F24 Activation records are stored on _**run time stack**_.

F25 Subprogram exemplifies _**process**_ abstraction.

F26 The two fundamental kinds of subprograms are _**functions**_ and _**procedures**_.

F27 A _**coroutine**_ is a special subprogram that has multiple entry points.

F28 Subprograms that return a value are called _**functions**_, and those that do not return a value are called _**procedures**_.

F29 Local variables in the C family of languages are (by default) allocated as _**stack–dynamic**_ variables.

F30   The parameter passing mechanism, where the values of the actual parameters are copied onto the formal parameters is called ***pass–by–value***.

F31   In most contemporary languages, parameter passing takes place via the ***stack*** data structure.

F32   A(n) ***overloaded*** subprogram has the same name as another subprogram in the same referencing environment.

F33   C / C++ does not allow ***arrays*** and ***functions*** as return types in functions.

F34   A subprogram whose execution has begun but not yet terminated is said to be ***active***.

F35   A function that takes one or more functions as arguments, or/and returns a function as its result, is known as ***higher-order*** function.

F36   The evaluation of actual parameters (arguments) before calling the function is known as ***eager*** evaluation.

F37   The evaluation of actual parameters (arguments) only if it is needed, or only to the extent needed is known as ***lazy*** evaluation.

F38   The actual parameters are not changed the ***pass-by-value*** parameter passing.

F39   More than one formal parameter referring to the same object is known as ***aliasing***.

F40   Subprograms which retain (some or all) state information across invocations are known as ***history-sensitive***.

F41   For history-sensitive subprograms (some or all) local variables must be declared with the `static` keyword.

F42   A local variable of subprogram can retain its value across different invocations when declared with the keyword `static`.

F43   A subprogram and its referencing environment, are together known as, a ***closure***.

F44 When a subprogram returns, the values of the formal parameters are copied to the actual parameters in the **_out_** and **_in-out_** mode of parameter passing.

F45 The non-code part of a subprogram consisting of parameters, local variables, and return address (among a few other things) is collectively called **_activation record_**.

F46 The main items of a subprogram's activation record are **_parameters_**, **_local variables_**, and **_return address_**.

F47 The addresses of the subprograms which are called are determined by the **_linker / loader_**.

F48 Languages which do not support **_stack-dynamic_** variables cannot support recursion.

F49 Subprogram parameters are (commonly) passed via **_registers_** in RISC machines.

IOIOIOIOIOIOIOIOIOIOIOIOIOIOIOIOIOIOIOIOIOIOIOIOIOIOIOIOI

Essay-type Questions

F1 How is the exact type of operation determined in case of overloaded operators?
The exact type of operation in the case of an overloaded operator is determined by the types of its operands.

F2 In Ruby, when a return statement has multiple expressions, how are the values of the expressions returned?
An array of the values of all the expressions is returned.

F3 What is meant by subprograms being used as first-class objects?
This means that subprograms assigned to variables, passed as parameters, and returned from functions.

F4 What is an overloaded subprogram?
It is a subprogram that has the same name as another subprogram in the same referencing environment.

F5 What are the main items in the activation record?

The main items in the activation record are:
1. Local variables of the procedure call
2. Return address
3. The actual parameters passed to the procedure call

F6   What is the return address that is part of an activation record?
The return address is the address of the statement following the procedure call.

F7   What are the advantages and disadvantages of parameters passed only by reference?

The main advantage is the fast accesses to formal parameters in subprograms, since it avoids the overhead of copying. The disadvantages are that recursive functions are not easy/natural to implement. It also leads to aliasing problems.

F8   What is the *protocol* of a subprogram?
The protocol of a function is its *parameter profile* – consisting of number, order, and types of the formal parameters, and its return type.

F9   Briefly describe *pass–by–value–result*.
This is an implementation model for in-out mode parameters. The actual parameter values are copied onto the formal parameters (similar to pass–by–value) at the time of function call, and the values of the formal parameters are copied back to the actual parameters (similar to pass–by–result) at the time of return from the function call.

F10   When would a global variable not be visible inside a subprogram?
When a variable with the same name as a global variable is declared in the subprogram

F11   What are the disadvantages of pass-by-name parameter passing?
Programs that use pass-by-name parameters can be complex and difficult to understand. Also, pass-by-name is far less efficient than other parameter passing methods.

F12   Why are nested subprograms not allowed in several languages?
Many contemporary languages provide better ways to organize programs. Also, nesting of subprograms reduces the writability and readability of programs.

F13 What is meant by 'functions treated as first-class objects' in a programming language?

A programming language is said to treat functions as first-class objects if it supports:

1. Passing functions as arguments to other functions
2. Returning them as the values from other functions
3. Assigning them to variables
4. Storing them in data structures

IOIOIOIOIOIOIOIOIOIOIOIOIOIOIOIOIOIOIOIOIOIOIOIOIOIOIOIOI

G. Object-Oriented Programming

True/False Questions

G1   A derived class cannot add variable(s) to those inherited from its base class. *False*

G2   A derived class can add method(s) to those inherited from its base class. *True*

G3   A derived class cannot modify the behavior of its inherited methods. *False*
[The derived class may modify the methods inherited from the base class to suit the objects of the derived class]

G4   A modified method of a derived class cannot have the same name as its parent's method. *False*

G5   All of the variables of a base class will be visible in its derived classes. *False*
[Variables declared in the base class to have private access are not visible in the derived classes]

G6   All of the methods of a base class may not be visible in its derived classes. *True*
[Methods declared in the base class to have private access are not visible in the derived classes]

G7   Instance variables are associated with a class. *False*
[Instance variables are associated with objects, which are instances of a class]

G8   Class variables are associated with a class. *True*

G9   Class methods can perform operations only on the class. *False*
[Class methods can perform operations both on the class and on objects of the class]

G10 A graph is required to represent the relationship among several derived classes and the base classes in the case of single inheritance. *False*
[A tree is adequate since any derived class in single inheritance can only have one base class (parent)]

G11 A tree may not be adequate to represent the relationship among a derived class and the base classes in the case of multiple inheritance. **True**
[A derived class would have multiple base classes (parents) in multiple inheritance]

G12 All abstract classes must be completely independent. **False**
[Inheritance creates dependencies between base and derived classes]

G13 Private members of a base class are visible to its derived classes. **False**

G14 An abstract class cannot be instantiated. **True**

G15 An abstract class cannot be subclasses. **False**

G16 The invocation of methods of object-oriented languages is slower than the invocation of subprograms of imperative languages. **True**
[The methods of object-oriented languages are invoked by the use of message passing which adds some overhead]

G17 Operations to be applied to variables which could be bound to different types at runtime can be handled by static polymorphism. **False**
[Since the types of objects that the variables are bound to, are known only at runtime, dynamic polymorphism is necessary]

G18 In static polymorphism, the actual method to be invoked can be resolved at compile time. **True**

G19 In dynamic polymorphism, the actual method to be invoked cannot be resolved at compile time, but only at runtime. **True**

G20 Method overloading is valid for methods not in the same class. **False**
[Method overloading is valid only for methods in the same class]

G21 Method overriding is valid for methods in different classes. **False**
[Method overriding is valid across classes with inheritance relationship]

G22 In method overloading the signature (number and type of arguments) of the methods must be different. **True**

G23 In method overriding the signature (number and type of arguments) of the methods could be different. **False**
[In method overriding, method signatures must be same]

G24 In method overloading the return types of the methods must be the same. **_False_**
[The return types of the methods could be different in method overloading]

G25 Overloaded functions/methods are in the same scope. **_True_**

G26 Overridden functions/methods are in different scopes. **_True_**

G27 Polymorphism is the process to define more than one body for functions/methods with same name.

G28 Method overriding can be viewed as polymorphism. **_True_**

G29 Both method overloading and overriding can be viewed as providing polymorphism. **_True_**

G30 In a single-inheritance object-oriented language, a class may have any number of base classes. **_False_**
[A class can have at most one base (parent) class]

G31 In a single-inheritance object-oriented language, a class may have any number of superclasses. **_True_**

G32 In a single-inheritance object-oriented language, a class may have any number of derived classes. **_True_**

G33 The private components of an object are accessible to all objects of the same class. **_True_**
[Note that a private component of an object is different from that of a class]

G34 Polymorphism can be either static or dynamic. **_True_**

G35 In C++, an abstract class may not have completely defined methods. **_False_**
[An abstract class in C++ may have completely defined methods. However, it must have at least one pure virtual function]

G36 In C++, a class need not have a parent class. **_True_**

G37 C++ does not allow the abstract data types to be parameterized. **_False_**

G38 C# structs do not support inheritance. **_True_**

G39 In C++, class instances can only be heap dynamic (and not stack dynamic). *False*

G40 In C++, the member functions of a class must defined within the class definition. *False*
[The member functions of a class may be defined either inside or outside the class definition]

G41 Object-oriented languages such as C++ and Java do not support message passing. *False*

G42 In Java, there is no explicit object deallocation. *True*

G43 In C++, constructors and destructors can be defined for any class. *True*

G44 In C++, method bindings can only be static. *False*
[In C++, the method bindings can be either static or dynamic]

G45 In C++, objects can only be heap dynamic. *False*
[In C++, objects can be any of static, stack dynamic, or heap dynamic]

G46 In C++, conversion from a value of a base type to a value of a derived type is allowed. *False*

G47 C++ includes no predefined exceptions. *True*

G48 In C++, the catch function can have only a single formal parameter. *True*

G49 In C++, all of the instances of a class share a single copy of the member functions. *True*

G50 In C++, each instance of a class has its own copy of the class data members. *True*

G51 In C++, an abstract class contains at least one pure virtual function. *True*

G52 In C++, a pure virtual function cannot be called. *True*

G53 In C++, a function name can be overloaded even if the functions with that name have the same signature. *False*
[The function name can be overloaded only when the functions with that name have different signature]

G54 An instance of a class is known as ***object***.

G55 In C++, **cin** and **cout** are ***statements*** and **>>** and **<<** are ***operators***.

G56 In C++, objects (non-primitive types) cab be directly printed using the **<<** operator. ***False***

G57 In C++, the **<<** I/O operator cannot be overload to support printing the class objects. ***False***

G58 In C++, it is not possible to declare pointers to class objects. ***False***

G59 In C++, all class instances are heap dynamic. ***False***
[In C++, the class instances can be either stack or heap dynamic]

G60 C++ has no encapsulation construct. ***True***

G61 C++ constructors cannot be overloaded. ***False***
[Constructors can be overloaded as long as each of the constructors have a unique parameter profile]

G62 In C++, constructors and destructors do not have return types nor do they return values. ***True***

G63 In C++, references and pointers can be used on constructors and destructors. ***False***

G64 In C++, constructors can be declared with the keyword **virtual**. ***False***

G65 In C++, constructors and destructors cannot be declared **static**, **const**, or **volatile**. ***True***

G66 C++ provides garbage collection (implicit reclamation of unreferenced storage). ***False***

G67 In C++, constructors and destructors obey the same access rules as member functions. ***True***

G68 In C++, storage allocated to objects can only be reclaimed by explicit call to **delete**. ***False***

[The destructor function is invoked automatically when an object goes out of scope. Explicitly allocated storage using the **new** operator is reclaimed by the use of **delete**]

G69　In C++, derived classes inherit constructors / destructors from their base classes. *False*

G70　In C++, constructors can be overloaded. *True*

G71　In C++, destructors can be overloaded. *False*

G72　In C++, derived classes may call the constructor and destructor of base classes. *True*

G73　In C++, non-inlined methods must be defined outside the class. *True*

G74　In Java, objects are accessed through reference variables. *True*

G75　In Java, a class need not have a parent class. *False*
[In Java, all classes are subclasses of a 'root' class called **Object**]

G76　In Java, objects can be either stack dynamic or heap dynamic. *False*
[In Java, objects are heap dynamic]

G77　In Java, method bindings can only be dynamic. *False*
[In Java, the method bindings can be either static or dynamic]

G78　Java has friend functions and friend classes. *False*

G79　In Java, all objects (class instances) are heap dynamic. *True*

IOIOIOIOIOIOIOIOIOIOIOIOIOIOIOIOIOIOIOIOIOIOIOIOIOIOIOIOI

Fill-in the-blanks Questions

G1　In object-oriented languages the data abstraction construct is known as *class*.

G2　The variables and methods (subprograms) of a class are together called *members*.

G3   The members of a class that are visible only within the class are known as *private* members.

G4   The members of a class that are visible in its derived class are known as *public* members.

G5   In *pure object-oriented* languages, all computation is initiated via message passing.

G6   A class that is independent (not defined or derived from other classes) is known as *base class* (or *super class* or *parent class*).

G7   A class (some of) whose components are inherited from some other class is known as *derived class* (or *subclass* or *child class*).

G8   A class from which a new class is derived is called *base* (or *parent* or *super*) class.

G9   *Object* is an instance of an abstract data type.

G10 A method of a class with only the protocol, but without a definition (body) is known as *abstract* method.

G11 A class with at least one abstract method is known as *abstract* class.

G12 Deriving a class from several base classes is called *multiple inheritance*.

G13 The number and type of arguments associated with a method are referred to as its *signature*.

G14 In method *overloading*, methods must have same name and different signature (number and type of arguments).

G15 In method *overriding*, methods must have same name and same signature.

G16 Method *overloading* is considered compile time polymorphism.

G17 Method *overriding* is considered runtime polymorphism.

G18 The resolution of the appropriate operations to be applied to variables at run-time is known as *dynamic* polymorphism.

G19 The functions and procedures that can operate upon the data members of a class are known as ***methods***.

G20 The collection of all methods of a class is known as the class's ***message interface***.

G21 The calls to methods are sometimes referred to as ***messages***.

G22 The process of modifying a method in a derived class that has been inherited from a base class is known as ***overriding***.

G23 The method of a derived class which is inherited from a base class that is modified is known as ***overridden*** method.

G24 The broad kinds of variables provided by classes are ***instance*** variables and ***class*** variables.

G25 The broad kinds of methods provided by classes are ***instance*** methods and ***class*** methods.

G26 The ***instance*** variables are associated with objects.

G27 The ***instance*** variables of a class store the state of an object of the class.

G28 There is only one copy of ***class*** variables for a class.

G29 ***Instance*** methods operate only on the objects of a class.

G30 ***Class*** methods can perform operations both on the class and on objects of the class.

G31 A class derived from more than one base class is said to have ***multiple*** inheritance.

G32 The same method name overloaded with different type or number of parameters in same class is allowed in ***static*** polymorphism.

G33 In static polymorphism, the actual method to be invoked is resolved at ***compile*** time.

G34 The same method overridden with same signature in different classes is allowed in ***dynamic*** polymorphism.

G35   In **_dynamic_** polymorphism, the actual method to be invoked can only be resolved at runtime.

G36   The facility which supports a collection of logically related code and data to be organized and independently compiled is known as **_encapsulation_**.

G37   A collection of classes and methods that are individually linked to an executing program, as needed during execution, is known as **_dynamic linked library (DLL)_**.

G38   The association between a method and its class is contained in a table known as **_dispatch table_**.

G39   In static polymorphism, the multiple forms are resolved at **_compile_** time.

G40   In C++, variables which are declared in another namespace can be accessed by using the **_:: scope_** operator.

G41   In C++, special kind of parameter that can be used to pass a type as argument is known as **_template parameter_**.

G42   In C++, a member of a class that can be redefined in its derived classes is known as a **_virtual_** member.

G43   In C++, a class that declares or inherits a virtual function is known as a **_polymorphic_** class.

G44   In C++, late binding of a method is achieved by the use of the **_virtual_** keyword in a method's declaration.

G45   The objects of a(n) **_immutable_** class cannot be modified.

G46   In C++, data abstraction is provided by **_classes_**.

G47   In C++, the access specifiers are **_private_**, **_public_** and **_protected_**.

G48   In C++, the member function of a class which has no definition is known as **_pure virtual_** function.

G49   In C++, a function not defined in a class, but which can access the non-public members of a class is known as **_friend_** function.

G50 C++ supports parameterized ADTs through its *templated* classes.

G51 In C++, heap allocated objects are explicitly deallocated using the `delete` method.

G52 In C++, *friend* subprograms or classes have full access to private data and operations of the class.

G53 In C++, the implicit conversion of a value of a derived class to a value of its base class is called *up* or *narrowing* conversion.

G54 In C++, a *public* component is accessible to any user of the class.

G55 In C++, *protected* component is accessible within the class as well as within a class derived from it.

G56 In C++, a *private* component is accessible only within the class.

G57 In C++, the inlining of methods eliminates the cost of *linkage*.

G58 In Java, only *primitive scalar (Boolean, character, numeric)* types are not objects.

G59 Java objects are allocated on the *heap*.

G60 In Java, all classes are descendants of the `Object` class.

G61 In Java, a method that is defined to be `final` cannot be overridden in any descendant class.

IOIOIOIOIOIOIOIOIOIOIOIOIOIOIOIOIOIOIOIOIOIOIOIOIOIOI

Essay-type Questions

G1 What is a class?
A class is like a 'template' or somewhat roughly like datatype. It is made up of two components – (a) data members and (b) methods (which are subprograms). It defines the structure and behavior of objects, which are instances of the class.

G2 What are the similarities between subprograms (of procedural languages) and methods (of object-oriented languages)?

Both are similar in terms of having block(s) of executable code, taking arguments (actual parameters), doing computation, and returning results.

G3   What are the differences between subprograms (of procedural languages) and methods (of object-oriented languages)?
The subprogram is invoked by a call from a calling subprogram. Thus the invocation from another subprogram can be viewed as procedural. Also, a subprogram operates on any data local or non-local. A method invocation occurs via a message sent to an object to execute that method. In this sense, the invocation of a method can be viewed as being done by the object, based upon a received message. A method (usually) operates on the data of the class in which it is defined.

G4   Why cannot the actual method to be invoked in dynamic polymorphism be determined at compile time?
The type of object(s) on which method is being invoked is not known at compile time but will be known only at run time.

G5   What is a major problem with multiple inheritance?
A major problem with multiple inheritance is that two of the base classes (parent classes) may define methods with the same name and the same protocol. This causes ambiguities by multiply-defined components across the parent classes. The derived (sub) class must possibly re-implement those methods or explicitly resolve using the scope resolution operator in order to avoid the name conflicts.

G6   What are the benefits provided by inheritance in ADTs (Abstract Data Types)?
Inheritance makes reuse of abstract data types much easier, because with inheritance, the modifications of existing types need not be done on the legacy code. Inheritance supports natural object hierarchies.

IOIOIOIOIOIOIOIOIOIOIOIOIOIOIOIOIOIOIOIOIOIOIOIOIOIOIOIOI

H. Exception Handling

True/False Questions

H1   An exception is a run-time condition. ***True***

H2   All exceptions are errors. ***False***
[Exceptions can also be used to return status information, not just error conditions]

H3   All errors detectable by compilers are detected by the hardware. ***False***
[Array subscript (index) going out of bounds are detected by several languages, but almost never by the hardware]

H4   Checks for array subscript (index) going out of bounds is provided by all languages. ***False***
[C does not provide subscript range checks]

H5   Exceptions cannot be handled in languages that do not have built-in exception handling facility. ***False***
[User-defined exception handlers can be provided]

H6   In C++, an exception handler may re-throw the exception to be intercepted by another handler. ***True***

H7   In C++, there is no direct way to access the object thrown during an exception that is caught by a `catch(...)` block. ***True***

H8   In C++, the programmer cannot implement one's own `unexpected()` function. ***False***

H9   In C++, the `unexpected()` function (when called on unspecified exception), can further throw an exception. ***True***

H10   In C++, a `terminate()` function can never return to its caller. ***True***

H11   In C++, the inherited subprograms in the derived class cannot be overridden by redefining the subprogram. ***False***

H12 In C++, a programmer defined function can be called when an exception is not handled. ***True***

H13 In C++, all thrown errors can be caught and successfully dealt with by a catch block. ***False***

H14 C++ exceptions cannot be user-defined class. ***False***

H15 In C++, any object can be thrown, including the object that caused the exception. ***True***

H16 In C++, the `catch(...)` must be the last catch block. ***True***

H17 In C++, `try` block must be accompanied by one or more `catch` blocks. ***True***

H18 Java provides some default exception handlers. ***False***

H19 In Java, a method must declare all exceptions that it can possibly throw. ***True***

H20 In Java, unchecked exceptions can be thrown by any method. ***True***

H21 In Java, user programs cannot define their own exception classes. ***False***

IOIOIOIOIOIOIOIOIOIOIOIOIOIOIOIOIOIOIOIOIOIOIOIOIOIOIOIOI

Fill-in the-blanks Questions

H1 During program execution, a condition requiring special processing is known as ***exception***.

H2 Run-time anomalies or abnormal conditions encountered by a program during its execution are known as ***exceptions***.

H3 The special processing required of an exception condition is commonly known as ***exception handling***.

H4 In C, the `setjmp/longjmp` facility enables defining additional points within the program that the exception handler can return to.

H5　In C++, the **throw** statement causes an exception to be raised.

H6　In C++, the **try** block identifies the scope of a sequence of statements for which exception handlers are active.

H7　In C++, the **catch** block contains the exception handler.

H8　In C++, the decision made at compile-time whether to call the inherited subprogram or the newly defined subprogram is called *static binding* (**or** *early binding*).

H9　In C++, a *catch* block implements an exception handler.

H10　In C++, the **catch(...)** must be the last catch block.

H11　In C++, the **finally** clause handles the exception when no catch is used.

H12　In C++, the **catch(...)** handler catches all thrown exceptions that have not been caught by a previous catch block.

H13　In C++, the default implementation of **unexpected()** calls **terminate()**.

H14　In C++, a thrown exception that is not listed in the exception specification, the library function that is called to handle it is **unexpected()**.

H15　In C++, a **catch** block follows immediately after a **try** statement or immediately after another **catch** block.

H16　In C++, an exception handler is implemented in a **catch** block.

H17　In Java, the two categories of exception are *checked* and *unchecked*.

H18　In Java, unchecked exceptions are of class **Error** and **RuntimeException** and their descendants.

H19　In Java, all exceptions are objects of classes that are descendants of the **Throwable** class.

H20　In Java, the super class of all exceptions is the **Throwable** class.

H21 In Java, the two predefined exception classes (subclasses of **Throwable**) are **Error** and **Exception**.

H22 In Java, errors that are thrown by the run-time system are associated with the **Error** exception class and its descendants.

H23 In Java, the keywords related to exception handling are **try**, **catch**, **throws**, **throw** and **finally**.

H24 In Java, the statements that may throw exceptions are in the **try** block.

H25 In Java, the keyword for declaring an exception is **throws**.

H26 In Java, the keyword for (manually) throwing an exception is **throw**.

H27 In Java, if an exception occurs, it is caught and handled (processed) by the **catch** block.

H28 In Java, the operator used to create instance of an exception is **new**.

IOIOIOIOIOIOIOIOIOIOIOIOIOIOIOIOIOIOIOIOIOIOIOIOIOIOIOIOIOI

Essay-type Questions

H1 Give examples of exceptions.
Some examples of exception conditions are, (a) divide by zero, (b) arithmetic overflow/underflow, (c) illegal memory address, (d) invalid op code in instruction, and (e) accessing a NULL pointer.

H2 List some advantages of support for exception handling in a programming language.
1. Exception handling facility helps in keeping the error-handling code separate from the essential computation, thus enhancing readability.
2. It allows several different errors to be handled by a single section of code.
3. It reduces the burden on the programmer to make various checks (ex. range check for arrays), with the compiler inserting machine code for several checks.

4. It enables detection and handling of conditions which are unforeseen by the programmer.

H3 Give the C++ keywords along with their purpose for handling exceptions.
The C++ keywords for handling exceptions are the following.
try: Represents a block of code that can throw an exception.
catch: Represents a block of code that is executed when a particular exception is thrown.
throw: Used to throw an exception. It is also used to list the exceptions that a function throws, but does not handle itself.

H4 In C++, where are the allowable objects that a function can catch declared?
The allowable objects that a function can catch are declared in the parentheses following the **catch** keyword.

H5 In C++, what are the types of objects that can be caught during exception?
In C++, the object types that can be caught during exception are:
1. objects of the fundamental types,
2. **const** and **volatile** types
3. base class objects
4. derived class objects
5. references and pointers to the above types

H6 In C++, list the scenarios when **terminate()** is called.
In C++, the **terminate()** call occurs in any of the following scenarios:
1. When **terminate()** is explicitly called
2. When no catch can be matched to a thrown object
3. When a system defined **unexpected()** is called
4. When the stack becomes corrupted during the exception-handling process

H7 What are the C++ language constructs for handling exceptions?
C++ provides three language constructs to implement exception handling:
1. Try blocks
2. Catch blocks
3. Throw expressions

H8 Briefly describe the control flow in the **catch** blocks in C++.

One or more **catch** blocks are defined immediately following the **try** block. Each **catch** block identifies what type or class of objects it can catch.

1. If the object thrown matches the type of a catch expression, control passes to that **catch** block.
2. If the object thrown does not match the first **catch** block, subsequent **catch** blocks are searched for a matching type.
3. If no match is found, the search continues in all enclosing **try** blocks and subsequently in the code that called the current function.
4. If no match is found after all **try** blocks are searched, a call to terminate() is made.

H9 Describe the structure and function of a **catch** block in Java.

In Java, a **catch** block starts with the keyword **catch** followed by a parenthesized exception declaration containing optional qualifiers, a type, and an optional variable name. The declaration specifies the type of object that the exception handler may catch. Once an exception is caught, the body of the catch block is executed. If no handler catches an exception, the program is terminated.

H10 Describe the exception handling constructs in C++.

C++ uses a special construct (similar to a compound statement) which is defined by the reserved word **try** and specifies the scope for exception handlers. Each exception handler is defined using a function named with the **catch** keyword. The handler can have only a single formal parameter. A handler with ellipsis (...) as the formal parameter acts as the "catch-all" handler which handles all exceptions for which no handler was found or defined. The exception handlers can have any C++ code.

H11 Describe the exception handling constructs in Java.

In Java, all exceptions are objects of classes that are derived from **Throwable** class. There are two pre-defined exception classes namely (a) **Error** and (b) **Exception**. **Error** classes are related to errors thrown by the Java run-time system (and not user programs). The **Exception** classes are related to I/O exceptions and run-time errors of user programs. User programs can define their own exception classes.

H12 In Java, which part of code gets executed whether exception is caught or not?

The **finally** block of the code gets executed whether exception is caught or not. The closing of files, database connection, etc., are usually done in **finally** block.

IOIOIOIOIOIOIOIOIOIOIOIOIOIOIOIOIOIOIOIOIOIOIOIOIOIOIOIOIOI

I. Languages and Features

True/False Questions

I1   The variables in BASIC do not have explicit types. ***True***

I2   In Smalltalk, all objects are allocated on the heap. ***True***

I3   Smalltalk has an explicit deallocation operation to delete objects. ***False***

I4   COBOL supports dynamic data structures. ***False***

I5   COBOL supports recursion. ***False***

I6   In Ada, casts have the syntax of function calls. ***True***

I7   Ada packages cannot be compiled separately. ***False***

I8   Type checks and array bounds are not done in C. ***True***

I9   In C/C++, the pre-processor directives cannot be used to create macros. ***False***

I10 The '*' operator in C/C++ has operation(s) other than multiplication. ***True***

I11 In C, storage for a variable of non-primitive type must always be explicitly allocated by the use of some 'allocation' operator. ***False***
[In C, just declaration of a variable of non-primitive type allocates a block of memory of the required size]

I12 In C, I/O functions are not supported by the basic language constructs. ***True***
[In C, I/O functions, string manipulations, and several mathematical functions are supported by library routines]

I13 In C, string is not a basic (primitive) datatype. ***True***

I14 C does not have (explicit) Boolean data type. ***True***

I15 C supports (explicit) String data type. ***False***

I16   C/C++ does not have array-bounds checks. ***True***

I17   In C/C++, files containing one or more subprograms can be independently compiled. ***True***

I18   C++ has garbage collection mechanism. ***False***

I19   C++ provides no operations on enumeration types. ***True***

I20   In C#, the pre-processor directives can be used to create macros. ***False***

I21   In C#, the pre-processor directives can be used for conditional compilation. ***True***

I22   Java is a type-safe language. ***True***

I23   Java bytecode can only be compiled, and not interpreted, into native code at run time. ***False***

I24   In Java, a class should always contain a no-arg constructor. ***False***

I25   In Java's Math class, all methods are static. ***True***

I26   In Java, the constructors must always be public. ***False***

I27   In Java, the constructors of a class may be protected. ***True***

I28   Java does not have array-bounds checks. ***False***

I29   Java does not have a pre-processor. ***True***

I30   Java does not support macros. ***True***

I31   Java has no pointer data type. ***True***

I32   In Java, a default constructor is automatically provided if no constructors are explicitly declared in the class. ***True***

I33   In Java, at least one constructor must always be defined explicitly for a class. ***False***

I34   In Java, every class provides a default constructor. ***False***

I35   In Java, the default constructor is a no-arg constructor. ***True***

I36   In Java, multiple constructors cannot be defined in a class. ***False***

I37   In Java, constructors do not have a return type (including void). ***True***

I38   In Java, constructors must have the same name as the class itself. ***True***

I39   In Java, whenever a variable of non-primitive type is declared, a block of memory of the required size is allocated. ***False***

I40   In Java, the methods or data members declared as *protected* are accessible within same package but not in sub classes in different package. ***False***

I41   In Java, the static method exists even before an object of a defined class is created. ***True***

I42   In Java, more than one variable-length parameter may be specified in a method. ***False***

I43   In Java, the variable-length parameter specified in a method must be the last parameter. ***True***

I44   In Java, the return type of a method could be a variable-length parameter. ***False***

I45   In Java, a non-static method can be called from a static method. ***False***

I46   In Java, a static method can be accessed from a non-static method. ***True***

I47   Java byte code does not hide machine-specific details. ***False***

I48   In Java, call-by-value is not used. ***False***

I49   A garbage collection mechanism is supported by the Java Virtual Machine (JVM). ***True***

I50   In Ruby, all instance variables are private by default, and that cannot be changed by the programmer. ***True***

I51   Ruby supports return of more than one value from a method. ***True***

I52   Ruby supports multiple inheritance. ***False***

I53   In Ruby, classes are dynamic (members can be added / deleted / changed during execution). ***True***

I54   In Ruby, the type of an object can be statically determined. ***False***

I55   In Ruby, even arithmetic, relational, and assignment operators are implemented as methods. ***True***

I56   In Ruby, there is no type checking of parameters. ***True***

I57   In Ruby, the formal parameters are typeless. ***True***

I58   In Python, the types of formal parameters must be specified. ***False***

I59   In Python, there is no type checking of parameters. ***True***

I60   The long integer type of Python can have unlimited length. ***True***

I61   Tuples in Python are mutable. ***False***

IOIOIOIOIOIOIOIOIOIOIOIOIOIOIOIOIOIOIOIOIOIOIOIOIOIOIOIOIOI

Fill-in the-blanks Questions

I1   The language in which all operators have equal precedence, and associate right-to-left is ***APL***.

I2   The language which uses a large range of special graphic symbols is ***APL***.

I3   The central datatype in APL is ***multidimensional array***.

I4   The central data structure in Scheme is ***list***.

I5   The single data type of Prolog is ***term***.
[Terms are either atoms, numbers, variables or compound terms]

I6   Record type was first introduced in the ***COBOL*** language.

I7   The language with the most reserved words is ***COBOL***.

I8   The encapsulation construct in Ada is called ***package***.

I9   In Ada related declarations of types, variables, and subprograms which are grouped together is known as ***package***.

I10   In ***JavaScript***, array subscripts / indices need not be contiguous.
[There is no storage allocated for the elements at the 'gaps' in the subscripts / indices]

I11   An early language developed for AI (artificial intelligence) applications is ***LISP***.

I12   The unary '*******' operator in C/C++ is used for the ***dereferencing*** operation.

I13   In C++, ***friend*** functions facilitate access to private members of a class.

I14   In C++, the operators **new** and **delete** manage ***heap*** storage.

I15   In C++, (the default) pointer whose value is the address of the object is **this**.

I16   In C#, a variable can have dynamic binding if declared with the reserved word **dynamic**.

I17   In ***C#*** language a variable with a **var** declaration must have an initial value.

I18   In Java, whenever a variable of non-primitive type is declared, a(n) ***implicit pointer*** is allocated.

I19   In Java, instance variables that are visible only in the class where they are defined are called ***private***.

I20   In Java, instance variables that are visible everywhere are called ***public***.

I21   In Java, instance variables that are visible in the class where they are defined and in all of the subclasses is called ***protected***.

I22   In Java, a method that is associated with a specific class is known as ***static*** method.

I23   In Java, a method that is associated with an object of a class is known as ***non-static*** or ***instance*** method.

I24   In Java, a ***package*** is a collection of classes.

I25   Associative arrays of Python are known as ***dictionaries***.

I26   The base class of all exception classes in Python is **Base-Exception**.

I27   In **_Ruby_** language, the arithmetic, relational, and assignment operators are implemented as methods.

I28   In Ruby, exceptions are explicitly raised with the **raise** method.

I29   Every exception class in Ruby has two methods, namely **message** and **backtrace**.

I30   All objects in Ruby are allocated on the **_heap_**.

I31   In Ruby, every exception clause has methods named **message** and **backtrace**.

I32   In Perl, scalar variable name begins with **$**, array name begins with **@**, and hash structure name begins with **%**.

I33   Associative arrays of Perl are known as **_hashes_**.

I34   A variable name must begin with a special character in the **_Perl_** programming language.

IOIOIOIOIOIOIOIOIOIOIOIOIOIOIOIOIOIOIOIOIOIOIOIOIOIOIOIOIOI

Essay-type Questions

I1   What is the role of modules in Fortran?
In Fortran, modules are the means for grouping related procedures and data together, and make them available to other program units. It can also enforce the accessibility to only specific parts of the module.

I2   What is the role of packages in Ada?
Packages in Ada broadly refer to a group of logically related subprograms along with their shared data. They facilitate modularization and separate compilation. By hiding the implementation details of the package from the programmer, it provides information hiding.

I3   What is the role of C++ namespace?
In C++, namespace facilitates grouping of entities like classes, objects and functions under a name. It is used to organize code into logical groups and to prevent name collisions, especially while using multiple libraries.

I4   What is the role of Java package?
In Java, a package broadly refers to a collection of related classes and interfaces. It facilitates organization of large programs into logical and manageable units.

I5   What are Python's modules and packages?
In Python, modules are essentially files containing definitions of classes and functions. A package can contain one or more relevant / related modules. Packages in Python provide a way of structuring the module namespace. For example, module A in packages P1 and P2 could be different, and referenced using P1.A and P2.A.

I6   What are Java's primitive types?
Java's primitive types are: boolean, char, byte, short, int, long, float, double.

I7   What are the different native data structures supported in Python?
Python has three kinds of data structures – (1) lists, (2) immutable lists (also called tuples), and (3) hashes (also called dictionaries)

I8   What are the roles of operators in Ruby?
Ruby is a pure object-oriented language, and every data value is an object. The operations are done by the methods. The operators are serve as syntactic mechanisms to specify methods for the corresponding operations.

I9   Give examples of languages which do not require declaration of variables before use.
BASIC, Perl, LISP, Scheme

I10 Give examples of languages which require declaration of variables before use.
C, C++, Java

I11 Give examples of languages which allow variable declarations to be anywhere a statement can be.
C++, C#, Java, JavaScript

I12 Give examples of languages which do not allow declaration of a variable in a nested block to have the same name as a variable in the enclosing block.
Java, C#

I13 Give examples of languages which do not have reserved keywords.
Fortran, PL/I, Lisp, Prolog

I14 Give examples of languages which support dynamic scoping.
APL, SNOBOL, Perl, Common Lisp

I15 Give examples of languages which support closures.
Lisp, Scheme, ML, Ruby, JavaScript, C#

I16 Give examples of languages which require the label of `goto` statements to be within the same procedure.
Ada, C

I17 Give examples of languages which have compound assignment operators (ex. +=).
C, C++, Java, Python, JavaScript, Perl, Ruby

I18 Give examples of languages which have (some) prefix operators.
Lisp, Scheme, Perl, C, C++, Java

I19 Give examples of languages where all operators are prefix operators.
Lisp, Scheme

I20 Give examples of languages which support conditional expressions (using '?' and ':' operators).
C, C++, Java, Perl, JavaScript, Ruby

I21 Give examples of languages which do not have multiple-selection statement.
Perl, Python

I22 Give examples of languages which have multiple-selection statement.
C, C++, Java, Fortran

I23 Give examples of languages which support use of arithmetic expressions as control expressions in conditional statements.
C, C++, Python

I24 Give examples of languages which support arrays of heterogeneous element types.
     Perl, Python, JavaScript, Ruby

I25 Give examples of languages which support array initializations at the time of allocation.
     C, C++, Java, C#

I26 Give examples of languages which specify array index range checks.
     Java, C#, Ada

I27 Give examples of languages which support array slices.
     Ada, Fortran, Perl, Python

I28 Give examples of languages which support expanding and shrinking arrays (which have already been allocated).
     Perl, JavaScript, Python, Ruby

I29 Give examples of languages which are (commonly) interpreted (not compiled).
     JavaScript, Ruby, Python, Perl, PHP

I30 Give examples of languages which store characters in 16–bit Unicode (UCS–2).
     C#, JavaScript, Python, Perl

I31 Give examples of languages which support **union** type.
     Pascal, Ada, C, C++

I32 Give examples of languages which support sets (unordered collections of distinct values from some ordinal type called base type).
     Pascal, Modula

I33 Give examples of languages which support **complex** numbers as built-in datatype.
     Fortran, Python, Common LISP, Scheme, Go

I34 Give examples of languages which support **complex** numbers via **libraries**.
     C, C++, Perl, Haskell

I35 Give examples of languages which provide **string** as a primitive type.
   Fortran, SNOBOL, Python

I36 Give examples of languages which support **decimal** datatype.
   COBOL, C#, F#

I37 Give examples of languages which have two sets of logical operators (**&&, and** ; **| |, or**).
   Perl, Ruby

I38 Give examples of languages which support enumeration types.
   Pascal, Ada, C, C++, C#, Java, Python

I39 Give examples of languages which support type inference (automatic detection of datatype based on context of use).
   C#, F#, Haskell, Java, ML

I40 Give examples of languages which support regular expressions.
   Perl (built-in); Java, Python, JavaScript, Ruby (via libraries)

I41 Give examples of languages which support nesting of classes.
   C++, Java, Python, Ruby, C#

I42 Give examples of pure object-oriented languages.
   Smalltalk, Ruby, Eiffel

I43 Give examples of languages which support multiple inheritance.
   C++, Python, Perl, Eiffel

I44 Give examples of languages (pure object-oriented or with object-oriented support) which do not directly support multiple inheritance.
   Smalltalk, Java, Ruby, C#

I45 Give examples of languages which support user-defined overloaded operators.
   Ada, C++, Python, Ruby, C#

I46 Give examples of languages which support subroutines with polymorphic parameters.
   Lisp, Smalltalk, ML, Haskell

I47 Give examples of languages which support parameters having default values (if no actual argument is passed during call).

C++, Python, Ruby, PHP

I48   Give examples of languages which support only stack-dynamic local variables in the methods.
C++, C#, Java, Python

I49   Give examples of languages which support user-defined aggregate data types (ex. arrays, structures).
Fortran, Cobol, C

I50   Give examples of languages in which methods are treated as objects and passed as parameters and returned from functions.
Python, Ruby

I51   Give examples of languages that support naming encapsulations.
Ada, C++, Java, C#, Ruby

I52   Give examples of languages which support concurrency.
Ada, C++, C#, Java, Python, Haskell

I53   Give examples of imperative languages which support object-oriented features.
C++, Java, C#, Python

I54   Give examples of languages which have built-in garbage collection.
LISP, Scheme, ML, Haskell, Ruby, Java, Python, Eiffel

I55   Give examples of languages which do not allow coercions in expressions.
ML, F#

I56   Give examples of languages in which only widening assignment coercions are done.
Java, C#

I57   Give examples of languages which support implicit type conversions.
C, C++, C#, Java, Python

I58   Give examples of languages which support explicit type conversions.
C, C++, C#, Java, Python

I59 Give examples of languages which support negative indices (subscripts).
Ada, Perl, Python, Ruby, Lua

I60 Give examples of languages which support character indices (subscripts).
Ada, Pascal

I61 Give examples of languages which allow the else-part of a conditional be optional.
Pascal, C, Java

I62 Give examples of object–oriented languages.
Ruby, Eiffel

I63 Give examples of scripting languages.
Perl, JavaScript, Ruby, VBScript, PHP

I64 Give examples of logic programming languages.
Prolog, ASP (answer set programming), Datalog

I65 Give examples of early languages developed for AI (artificial intelligence) applications.
LISP, Prolog

I66 Give examples of functional languages.
Lisp, Scheme, ML, Haskell

I67 Give examples of languages which use short circuit evaluation of Boolean expressions.
C, C++, Java, Python, Perl, Ruby

I68 Give examples of languages which do not do parameter type checking.
Perl, JavaScript, PHP, Python, Ruby

I69 Give examples of languages which allow return of multiple values from functions/methods.
Ruby, Python, ML, F#

I70 Give examples of languages which allow return values of any type from functions/methods.
Ada, Python, Ruby

I71   Give examples of languages where the assignment statement produces a result and can be used as an operand.
C, C++, Perl, JavaScript

I72   Give examples of languages which allow multiple-target multiple-source assignments
Perl, Ruby, Lua

I73   Give examples of languages which support *out mode* parameters.
Ada, Fortran, C#

I74   Give examples of languages which do not have the `goto` control structure.
Java, Python, Ruby

I75   Give examples of languages in which any numeric type value can be assigned to any numeric type variable.
Fortran, C, C++, Perl

I76   Give examples of languages which support imperative, object-oriented, and functional paradigms.
C++, C#, Java, JavaScript, Python, Fortran, Haskell, Ruby
[Note: The functional paradigm is mostly in the support for functions as first-class objects]

I77   Give examples of functional languages in which functions are treated as first-class objects.
Scheme, Common LISP, Haskell, ML

I78   Give examples of scripting languages in which functions are treated as first-class objects.
Perl, Python, JavaScript, Lua

I79   Give examples of languages in which functions (not the values returned) can be assigned to variables.
Python, Ruby

I80   Give examples of languages which have predefined overloaded subprograms.
C++, Java, C#

I81   Give examples of languages in which control expressions can be arithmetic.
C, C++

I82   Give examples of languages in which control expression must be Boolean.
Java, C#

I83   Give examples of languages which have labeled versions of `continue.`
Java, Perl

I84   Give examples of languages which allow mixed-mode expressions.
C++, Java, C#

I85   Give examples of languages which do not allow mixed-mode expressions.
Ada, ML, F#

I86   Give examples of procedural (imperative) languages.
Algol, Pascal, C, C++

I87   Give examples of languages that support pointers.
Ada, C, C++, Pascal, Fortran

I88   Give examples of languages that support pointer arithmetic.
C, C++

I89   Give examples of languages which support dynamic type binding of variables.
JavaScript, Python, Ruby, PHP

I90   Give examples of languages where there is no limit on the length of a variable name, and all characters are significant.
Ada, Java, C#

I91   Give examples of languages which require explicit declaration of variable type.
C, C++, Java, C#

I92   Give examples of languages which support implicit declaration of variable type.
Fortran, Python, Perl, Ruby

I93   Give examples of languages which perform type checks at compile time.
Ada, Pascal, C, C++, Java, C#

I94 Give examples of languages which perform type checks at runtime.
Smalltalk, Perl, Ruby, Python, JavaScript

I95 Give examples of languages which support heap-dynamic arrays.
Perl, JavaScript, Python, Ruby

I96 Give examples of languages which support nested subprogram definitions.
Ada, Fortran, Common LISP, Scheme, JavaScript, Python, Ruby

I97 Give examples of languages which do not support nested subprogram definitions.
C, C++, Java, Eiffel

I98 Give examples of languages which support associative arrays.
Python, Ruby, Perl

I99 Give examples of languages which support record types.
COBOL, C, C++, C#, Python, Ruby

I100 Give examples of languages which support strong typing.
Ada, Java, C#, ML, F#

I101 Give examples of languages which require all variables to have a declared type.
Ada, Pascal, C, Java

I102 Give examples of languages which have built-in pattern matching operations.
SNOBOL, Perl, Ruby JavaScript, PHP

I103 Give examples of languages which support pattern matching operations via libraries.
C++, C#, Java, Python

I104 Give examples of languages which support strings of fixed lengths (static lengths).
Java, Python, Ruby

I105 Give examples of languages which support strings of varying lengths with no maximum.
C++, JavaScript, Perl

I106 Give examples of languages which support reference types.
C++, C#, Java

I107 Give examples of languages which have built-in exponentiation operator.
Ada, Fortran, Python, Ruby, Perl

I108 Give examples of languages which do not have exponentiation operator.
C, C++, C#, Java

I109 Give examples of languages which support operator overloading.
Ada, Fortran, C++, C#, Python, Ruby, Haskell

I110 Give examples of languages which support polymorphism.
Java, C++, Python, Ruby

I111 Give examples of languages which support parameterized ADTs.
Ada, C++, C#, Java

I112 Give examples of languages which support implicit iterators over elements of a container object.
C++ Java, C#, Perl, Python, Ruby

I113 Give examples of languages which support dynamic scoping (in addition to static scoping) of variables.
Common LISP, Perl

I114 Give examples of languages which have built-in support for exception handling.
Ada, C++, C#, Java, Python, Ruby

IOIOIOIOIOIOIOIOIOIOIOIOIOIOIOIOIOIOIOIOIOIOIOIOIOIOIOIOIOIOIOIOI

J. Compilers

True/False Questions

J1　For an unambiguous grammar, the leftmost and the rightmost derivations produce different parse trees. *False*

J2　All syntax rules of a context free language can be specified in BNF. *False*

J3　The syntax analyzer is also commonly called the parser. *True*

J4　A terminal symbol could be on the LHS of a production rule of a grammar. *False*

J5　BNF is a meta–language commonly used to describe the syntax of a programming language. *True*

J6　The lexical analyzer is also commonly called the parser. *False*
[The lexical analyzer is also called scanner]

J7　Interpreted code generally runs faster than compiled code. *False*

J8　Lexical analyzers are usually developed as a function called by the syntax analyzer. *True*

J9　A non-terminal can appear on the RHS (Right Hand Side) of its definition. *True*

J10　A terminal symbol could be on the LHS of a production rule of a grammar. *False*

J11　*Java Bytecode* is the machine code which can be executed by the bare hardware. *False*
[Java Bytecode is intermediate code, not machine code]

J12　A sentence in a (programming) language could consist of non–terminal symbols. *False*

J13　Code optimization is a mandatory step in all compilers. *False*

J14 The descriptive power of EBNF is more than that of the corresponding BNF. *False*

J15 The nonterminal on the LHS of a production cannot appear on its RHS. *False*

J16 There could be more than one RHS for a given LHS of a production. *True*

J17 All syntax rules of a context free language can be specified in BNF. *False*

J18 Attribute grammars are used to specify the static semantics. *True*

J19 The lexical analyzer (scanner) can be (in most cases) automatically generated based on the regular expressions of the lexemes. *True*

J20 The output of the syntax analyzer is the input to the lexical analyzer. *False*

J21 Lexical analysis (scanning) precedes syntax analysis (parsing). *True*

J22 The output of the syntax analyzer is the input to the lexical analyzer. *False*

J23 EBNF is best suited for (implementing) recursive–descent parsers. *True*

J24 A recursive–descent parser produces a parse tree in bottom–up order. *False*
[A recursive–descent parser works in a top-down manner]

J25 Left recursion is not a problem for LR (bottom up) parsers. *True*

J26 There are ways of modifying a grammar to remove left recursion. *True*

J27 The parsing table of an LR parser can easily be produced manually (by hand). *False*
[The parsing table of an LR parser is usually produced automatically]

J28 The top of the parse stack of an LR parser always contains a state number. *True*

J29   Each of the different types of tokens (ex. numbers, variables, keywords) are described by its own regular expression. ***True***

J30   A left-linear grammar cannot be converted to a right-linear grammar. ***False***

J31   A language is regular if and only if it is accepted by finite automata. ***True***

J32   If a grammar has more than one leftmost (or rightmost) derivation the grammar is ambiguous. ***True***

J33   The intermediary nodes of the syntax tree are the tokens found by the lexical analysis. ***False***

J34   The leaves of the syntax tree read from left to right yields the same sequence as in the input text. ***True***

J35   The language $a^{20}b^{15}$ is regular. ***True***

J36   The language $\{a^n b^n \mid n \geq 0\}$ is regular. ***False***

J37   The language $a^* b^*$ is regular. ***True***

J38   The matching parentheses cannot be described by regular expressions. ***True***

J39   Every regular a language can be expressed by a grammar. ***True***

J40   Every grammar describes a regular language. ***False***

J41   LR parser (Left-to-right, Rightmost derivation) can recognize any deterministic context-free language in linear-bounded time. ***True***

J42   Canonical LR parser is no more powerful than LALR parser. ***False***

J43   Code optimization is carried out on the intermediate code rather than on the machine code. ***True***

J44   All finite languages are regular. ***True***

J45   All regular languages are finite. ***False***
      [The language corresponding to the regular expression **ab^{n}a**, $n \geq 0$ is regular, but infinite]

J46 A programming language which supports recursion can be implemented with static storage allocation. **_False_**

J47 Context-free grammars are adequate to describe all of the syntax of (most) programming languages. **_False_**

J48 The parsing algorithms of commercial compilers for programming languages have complexities less than $O(N^3)$. **_True_**

J49 Every regular grammar is LL(1). **_False_**

J50 Every regular set has a LR(1) grammar. **_True_**

J51 Left-recursive grammar is not suitable for predictive-parsing. **_True_**

J52 Context Free languages are accepted by finite automata. **_False_**
[Context Free languages are accepted by push-down automata]

J53 LR grammars are a restricted class of BNF grammars. **_True_**

J54 If a context free grammar G is ambiguous, the language L(G) generated by grammar G may or may not be ambiguous. **_True_**

J55 It is always possible to convert any ambiguous CFG to an unambiguous CFG. **_False_**

J56 Some ambiguous CFG can be converted to unambiguous CFG. **_True_**

J57 There always exists an unambiguous CFG corresponding to unambiguous context-free language (CFL). **_True_**

J58 Deterministic CFL may sometimes be ambiguous. **_False_**
[Deterministic CFL is unambiguous]

J59 Lexical analyzer is a finite automaton to recognize regular expressions. **_True_**

J60 An ambiguous grammar cannot be parsed by an LR(k) parser for any k. **_True_**

J61 An LR(k) grammar ($k > 1$) can be transformed into an LR(1) grammar. **_True_**

J62 LR(k) parser cannot recognize all deterministic context-free languages. ***False***

J63 Symbol table can be used for checking type compatibility. ***True***

J64 A bottom-up parser generates the left-most derivation. ***False***

J65 A bottom-up parser generates the right-most derivation in reverse. ***True***

J66 It is generally easier to compile declarative languages into efficient machine code than imperative languages. ***False***

J67 Lexical analysis can detect invalid / unexpected structure in programs. ***False***

J68 No production in a LL(1) grammar can be left-recursive. ***True***

J69 All lexemes (tokens) can be described by regular expressions. ***True***

J70 Lexical analysis must necessarily be recursive in order to handle nested parentheses. ***False***

J71 Balanced parenthesis cannot be described by regular expressions. ***True***

J72 Lexical analyzers do not need to have any knowledge of the grammar of a language for their correct operation. ***True***

J73 Finite State Machines may never have unlimited number of states. ***True***

J74 A successful parse of a program indicates that it is semantically correct. ***False***
[Parsing may not be able to detect correctness of all semantics of a program]

J75 Syntax analysis cannot handle type checking and type conversions. ***True***

J76 There are only a finite number of unambiguous non-LR(1) grammars. ***False***

J77 The root of the parse tree is the start symbol of derivation. ***True***

J78 LL parser can parse an ambiguous grammar. *False*

J79 SLR parser cannot parse an ambiguous grammar. *True*

J80 LR parser can parse an ambiguous grammar. *True*
[LR parser resolves the conflicts in parsing table based on operator precedence / associativity rules of the grammar.]

J81 The number of states of the SLR parser for a grammar has necessarily the same number of states as the LALR parser for the same grammar. *True*

J82 Syntax trees are a form of intermediate representation. *True*

J83 Syntax trees are commonly used during syntax and semantic analysis. *True*

J84 LALR parser is more powerful than SLR parser. *True*

J85 An operator precedence parser is a bottom-up parser that handles an operator-precedence grammar. *True*

J86 High-level language programs can be translated to different intermediate representations. *True*

J87 Compilers typically generate the executable with zero as the starting address. *True*

J88 Semantic analysis is done before parsing. *False*

J89 Optimization on the intermediate representation can be done before code generation. *True*

J90 Peephole optimization is usually done on the generated instructions. *True*

J91 Peephole optimization can never be done on the intermediate representation. *False*

J92 With the use of optimizing compiler, the order of the statements as executed may be different from the order in the source code. *True*

J93 The parse tree does not captures the associativity and the precedence of the operators. *False*

[Parse tree does capture the associativity and the precedence of the operators]

J94   A top-down parser cannot handle left recursive productions. **_True_**

J95   Some compilers produce only intermediate-level code instead of machine code. **_True_**

J96   In some systems, some parts of a program are compiled to machine code, and some parts to intermediate code. **_True_**

J97   The intermediate code produced by a compiler is always interpreted at runtime. **_False_**
[The intermediate code may be interpreted at runtime or converted to machine code by just-in-time compiler]

J98   It is never the case that in *any* system parts of a program are compiled to machine code, and parts are compiled to intermediate code. **_False_**

J99   Compiled code tends to be bigger than intermediate code. **_True_**
[Each of the intermediate code statements may expand to multiple machine language statements]

J100 Compilation of code into an intermediate language facilitates portability by hiding machine-specific details. **_True_**

J101 Left recursion is not a problem for LR parsers. **_True_**

J102 Unambiguous context-free grammars always generate a Deterministic context-free language (CFL). **_False_**

J103 Not every context-free language is deterministic. **_True_**

J104 Deterministic context-free languages (DCFL) are a proper subset of context-free languages. **_True_**

J105 Deterministic context-free languages (DCFLs) form a proper subset of unambiguous context-free languages (CFLs). **_True_**

J106 Some Deterministic Context Free Languages can be ambiguous. **_False_**

J107 Every unambiguous Context-Free Language (CFL) is accepted by a deterministic Pushdown Automaton (PDA). **_False_**

J108 Unambiguous grammars always generate deterministic Context-Free Languages (CFLs). *False*

J109 Any language generated by a Context-Free Grammar (CFG) can be recognized by a Pushdown Automaton (PDA). *True*

J110 Any language recognized by a Pushdown Automaton (PDA) can be generated by a Context-Free Grammar (CFG). *True*

J111 Every CFG has a corresponding PDA. *True*

J112 Every CFG has a corresponding deterministic PDA. *False*

J113 Any (regular) grammar constructed from a DFA will be LL(0). *True*

J114 In bottom-up parsing, the string to the right of the handle contains only terminals. *True*

J115 Type checking is done before parsing. *False*

J116 Type checking is done in the syntax analysis (parsing) phase of the compiler. *False*

J117 Type checking is done in syntax directed translation. *True*

J118 Checks for ensuring variable declarations before use can be described in the extended Backus–Naur form. *False*

J119 There exist some languages whose compilers can produce the object code in a single pass (of a compilation unit / source code). *True*

J120 Hashing cannot be used a method of organizing the symbol table. *False*

J121 Any context-free grammar can be modified in order to be parsable by the recursive-descent parser. *False*

J122 There is guarantee that any context-free grammar can be modified to be parsable by table-driven methods. *True*

J123 Every language that can be described by a regular expression can also be described by a grammar. *True*

J124 Every language that can be described by a grammar, can also be described by a regular expression. ***False***

J125 There are algorithms to remove both left recursion and common prefixes in grammars. ***True***

J126 A language may be LL(1) even though the grammar used to describe it is not. ***True***

J127 All grammars can be rewritten to allow LL(1) parsing. ***False***

J128 LL parser belongs to the class of bottom-up parsers. ***False***
[LL parser belongs to the class of top-down parsers]

J129 LL parser does not use backtracking. ***False***

J130 LR parsers belong to the class of bottom-up parsers. ***True***

J131 LR parsers accept a much larger class of grammars than LL parsers. ***True***

J132 Predictive parsers use backtracking. ***False***

J133 Recursive descent parsers do not use backtracking. ***False***

J134 Recursive descent parsers work bottom-up. ***False***
[Recursive descent parsers are top-down parsers and may use backtracking]

J135 Languages defined by regular grammars are a proper subset of the context-free languages. ***True***

J136 A non-recursive Context-Free Grammar (CFG) can generate infinite number of strings. ***False***

J137 Bottom-up parsing technique uses rightmost derivation. ***True***

J138 There is no backtracking in shift-reduce parsers. ***True***

J139 Leftmost and rightmost derivations could lead to different parse trees even in unambiguous grammar. ***False***
[The same parse tree results from both leftmost and rightmost derivations in unambiguous grammar]

J140 The LR parser can recognize any deterministic context-free language in linear time. ***True***

J141 The memory requirements of LR parser is about the same as those of SLR and LALR parsers. ***False***
[SLR and LALR parsers have much lower memory requirements than that of LR parser]

J142 The LALR parser is more powerful (in terms of language-recognition power) than the SLR parser. ***True***
[LALR parsers handle more grammars than SLR parsers]

J143 The LALR parser is less powerful (in terms of language-recognition power) than the CLR parser. ***True***
[Canonical LR parsers handle more grammars LALR parsers]

J144 LR parsers are no more powerful (in terms of the range of grammars handled) than LL parsers. ***False***
[LR parsers handle more grammars LL parsers]

J145 LALR parser does not need backtracking. ***True***

J146 LR parsers are deterministic. ***True***

J147 LR parser requires backtracking. ***False***

J148 LR parsers produce a parse in linear time. ***True***

J149 Bottom-up parsers can handle grammars that top-down parsers cannot handle. ***True***

J150 Bottom-up parsers build the parse tree from left to right. ***False***

J151 Leaves of a parse tree are the tokens generated by the lexical analyzer. ***True***

J152 Leaves of an abstract syntax tree are the tokens generated by the lexical analyzer. ***False***
[The leaves of an abstract syntax tree are the operands of an expressions, and the operators are internal nodes]

J153 The abstract syntax tree must be very closely tied to the grammar. ***False***
[The parse tree is very closely tied to the grammar]

J154 A token can have only one associated lexeme. *False*
[For example, several lexemes (variable names) could be associated with `identifier` token]

J155 For LR, LALR, and SLR parsers, the basic state machine is the same. *True*

J156 The parsing tables of LR, LALR, and SLR parsers are the same. *False*

J157 In left factoring, the common prefix must be a terminal. *False*

J158 In left factoring, the common prefix must be a non-terminal. *False*
[The common prefix may be a terminal or a non-terminal or a combination of both]

J159 Left factoring need not be done on grammars in order to be handled by LR parsers. *True*

J160 LR parsers can handle grammars with left recursion. *True*

J161 Left factoring need not be done on grammars in order to be handled by predictive parsers. *False*

J162 Top-down parsers cannot handle left recursion in grammars. *True*

J163 Predictive parsers can handle grammars with left recursion. *False*

J164 All ambiguous grammars have multiple choices of production for a nonterminal, causing conflicts during parsing. *True*

J165 Unambiguous grammars never cause conflicts (for the choice of production for a nonterminal) during parsing. *False*

J166 In predictive (top-down) parsing, there can be nonterminals to the left of the rewritten non-terminals. *False*

J167 There is no backtracking in an LL(1) parser. *True*

J168 A non-recursive Context-Free Grammar (CFG) can generate an infinite number of strings. *False*
[There must be a production with recursion in the grammar in order to generate infinite number of strings]

J169 Look-ahead of input symbols in LR parser avoids backtracking (or guessing). **_True_**

J170 A shift-reduce parser can parse the input text in one pass without backtracking. **_True_**

J171 The parsing table entries (cells) for a deterministic parser cannot have multiple, alternative actions. **_True_**

J172 The parse stack of the LR parser contains only grammar symbols. **_False_**
[It contains both the grammar symbols as well as the states]

J173 The top entry in the parse stack of an LR parser is always a state symbol. **_True_**

J174 Right linear grammar can be translated to a DFA (Deterministic Finite Automaton). **_True_**

J175 Left linear grammar cannot be translated to a DFA (Deterministic Finite Automaton). **_False_**
[Left linear grammar is transformed to right linear grammar, it's DFA is determined, and the resulting DFA is 'reversed' to obtain the DFA for the original left linear grammar]

IOIOIOIOIOIOIOIOIOIOIOIOIOIOIOIOIOIOIOIOIOIOIOIOIOIOIOIOI

Fill-in the-blanks Questions

J1   **_Language_** is the set of all strings over an alphabet.

J2   **_Grammar_** specifies rules for forming valid sentences.

J3   Every string of symbols in a derivation is called a **_sentential form_**.

J4   **_Attribute grammars_** enable additions to CFGs to carry some semantic info on parse tree nodes.

J5   An alphabet is a set of **_symbols_**.

J6   The set of all strings over an alphabet is called the **_language_**.

J7   The rules for forming valid sentences in a language is specified by its **_grammar_**.

J8   The smallest meaningful unit in the string representing a program is called *lexeme*.

J9   *Token* refers to the category of the smallest meaningful unit (lexeme) in a program.

J10 The *lexical analyzer (scanner)* breaks down the string representing a program into meaningful units.

J11 The process of converting a sequence of characters in the source code to tokens is known as *lexical analysis*.

J12 *Syntax* refers to the structure of program (units).

J13 *Semantics* refers to the meanings of program (units).

J14 The set of symbols and rules for generating a regular language is known as *regular grammar*.

J15 The compact algebraic notation which describes the set of all strings that are generated by a regular grammar is known as *regular expression*.

J16 The set of all strings generated by a regular grammar is known as *regular language*.

J17 *Regular languages* is the class of languages that can be generated by regular grammars / described by regular expressions / recognized by finite automata.

J18 The mechanism which recognizes/accepts the language generated by regular grammar is a *finite automaton*.

J19 *BNF (Backus–Naur Form)* is the universally used meta–language to describe the syntax of programming languages.

J20 The output of the lexical analysis phase of compiler is a set of *tokens*.

J21 The input to the syntax analyzer are the *tokens* which are output from the *lexical analyzer*.

J22 The output of the syntax analysis phase of compiler is the *parse tree*.

J23   ***Parse tree*** is a hierarchical (graphical) representation of a derivation using grammar rules.

J24   ***Attribute*** grammar can describe both the syntax and *static* semantics of a language.

J25   ***Grammar*** is a language generator.

J26   ***Parser*** is a language recognizer.
[The mechanism behind a parser is the pushdown automaton, which is commonly treated as the language recognizer]

J27   *BNF* stands for ***Backus–Naur Form***.

J28   The forms of the tokens of programming languages can be described by ***regular*** grammars.

J29   The syntax of programming languages can be described by ***context–free*** grammars.

J30   ***Lexemes (tokens)*** are the input to the syntax analyzer.

J31   Computing the attribute values of a parse tree is sometimes called ***decorating*** the parse tree.

J32   ***Dynamic semantics*** denote the meaning of the expressions, statements, and program units.

J33   The stage of compilation that is often optional is the ***code optimization*** phase.

J34   ***Pushdown automaton*** is the mathematical machine on which both top–down and bottom–up parsers are based.

J35   The mechanism which recognizes/accepts the language generated by Context-Free Grammar is known as ***Pushdown automaton***.

J36   The two primary operations (actions) of an LR parser are ***shift*** and ***reduce***.

J37   The keywords of a language are recognized during the ***lexical analysis*** phase of the compiler.

J38   In a compiler, the *symbol table* contains information about variables and their attributes.

J39   A *top-down* parser builds the parse tree starting with the start nonterminal.

J40   Recursive descent parsing belongs to the class of *top-down* parsing.

J41   Bottom-up parsing is also known as *shift reduce* parsing.

J42   Code optimizing transformations can be performed at *source* code and *intermediate* code levels.

J43   The automaton associated with BNF (Backus-Naur Form) grammar is the *pushdown* automaton.

J44   A Context-Free Language (CFL) is generated by a *context-free* grammar and is recognized/accepted by a *Pushdown Automata*.

J45   *Scanner generator* generates lexical analyzers from the input consisting of regular expression description of tokens of a language.

J46   *Parser generator* produces syntax analyzers (parsers) from input based on grammatical description of programming language (a context-free grammar).

J47   A context-free grammar that has at most one nonterminal in the RHS of each of its productions is known as a *linear grammar*.

J48   A grammar in which the non-terminal in RHS of the productions is at the left end is known as *left-linear (left-regular)* grammar.

J49   While parsing an input string, a top-down parser uses *leftmost* derivation.

J50   The outcome of the syntax analysis (parsing) stage is the *syntax tree*.

J51   The leaves of the syntax tree are the *tokens* (found by the lexical analysis).

J52   A Context-Free Grammar that has at most one non-terminal in the right hand side of each of its productions is known as *linear* grammar.

J53 The LR class of parsers in order of increasing power are **_SLR, LALR, CLR_**.

J54 The two parts of the parse table of LR parser are **_Action_** part and **_Goto_** part.

J55 For an entry in the Action part of the parse table, the row index is a **_state_** and the column index is a **_terminal symbol_**.

J56 For an entry in the Goto part of the parse table, the row index is a **_state_** and the column index is a **_nonterminal symbol_**.

J57 The possible entries in the Action part of the LR parse table are **_Shift, Reduce, Accept,_** and **_Error_**.

J58 The entries in the Goto part of the LR parse table are the **_states_**.

J59 The most commonly used data structure to maintain the state of a shift-reduce parser is **_stack_**.

J60 The top entry in the parse stack of an LR parser is always **_a state symbol_**.

J61 The process of using a compiler to compile itself is known as **_bootstrapping a compiler_**.

J62 **_Lexical generator_** is a program that takes a set of token definitions (each consisting of a regular expression and a token name) and generates a lexical analyzer.

J63 **_Separate compilation_** enables code reuse/libraries, parallel development and collaboration.

J64 The **_semantic analyzer_** adds annotations to the abstract syntax tree produced by the parser.

J65 **_Top-down_** parsing starts at the highest level of the parse tree and works down the parse tree by using the rules of grammar.

J66 **_Bottom-up_** parsing starts at the lowest level of the parse tree and works up the parse tree by using the rules of grammar.

J67 **_Top-down_** parsing attempts to find the leftmost derivations for an input string.

J68 ***Bottom-up*** parsing reduces the input string to the start symbol of a grammar.

J69 LL parsers belong to the class of ***top-down*** parsers.

J70 LR parsers belong to the class of ***bottom-up*** parsers.

J71 A compiler that recompiles only those portions of a program that have been modified is known as ***incremental*** compiler.

J72 The ***incremental*** compiler avoids wasteful recompiling of entire source code, where only a small portion of the code is changed.

J73 The technique where the intermediate representation of source code is compiled to native machine code at runtime is known as ***just-in-time compilation (JIT)***.

J74 An interpreter for a programming language written in that language itself is known as ***self-interpreter***.

J75 The process which allows a compiler to produce different executable programs based on parameters that are provided during compilation ***conditional compilation***.

J76 The process of applying the production rules of a grammar for obtaining the input string of the language is known as ***derivation***.

J77 Any initial part of a string w including the empty string and all of the symbols of w is known as the ***prefix*** of w.

J78 The number of prefixes of a string of length N is $\underline{\mathbf{N+1}}$.

J79 A ***suffix*** of a string is what remains of the string after a prefix has been taken off.

J80 A subsequence of a string is obtained by deleting any number of symbols from anywhere in the string. The subsequences of **abc** are **abc, bc, ac, ab, c, b, a,** and **ε**.

J81 The number of subsequences of a string of length N (with distinct symbols) is $\underline{\mathbf{2^N}}$.

J82 Errors that are not detected by the syntax analysis phase of the compiler are checked by the **_semantic analysis_** phase of the compiler.

J83 Type checking is done in the **_semantic analysis_** phase (part) of the compiler.

J84 The **_top-down_** parser uses leftmost derivation while parsing an input string.

J85 A compiler that translates a high-level language into another high-level language is called a **_source-to-source_** translator.

J86 A compiler that runs on platform (hardware/OS) and generates executable code for another platform (hardware/OS) is known as **_cross-compiler_**.

J87 Semantic analysis is also known as **_context sensitive analysis_**.

J88 **_Syntax-directed_** translation works by adding actions to the productions in a context-free grammar.

J89 The front-end of a typical compiler consists of **_lexical analysis_**, **_syntax analysis_**, **_semantic analysis_**, and **_intermediate code generation_** phases.

J90 The back-end of a typical compiler consists of **_code optimization_** and **_target code generation_** phases.

J91 **_Peephole optimization_** attempts to replace short sequences of instructions with a single, more efficient instruction.

J92 A grammar which leads to a situation where there is more than one correct parse tree for a given expression (statement) is known as **_ambiguous_**.

J93 A production of grammar where the leftmost variable of its RHS is same as non-terminal of its LHS is known as **_left recursive_**.

J94 A recursive descent parser is (usually) implemented based directly on **_the BNF description of syntax_**.

J95 The correct RHS to be selected from among more than one RHS in the reduction process of a bottom–up parser is known as **_handle_**.

J96 The leaf nodes of a parse tree correspond to the ***terminals*** of the grammar.

J97 The interior nodes of a parse tree correspond to the ***non-terminals*** of the grammar.

J98 ***In-order*** traversal of the parse tree gives the original input string.

J99 Parse tree is also known as ***derivation*** tree or ***concrete syntax*** tree.

J100 The interior nodes of the syntax tree represent ***operations***.

J101 The leaf nodes of the syntax tree represent ***operands*** (arguments of operations).

J102 A production of the form $A \rightarrow B$, where both A and B are single non-terminals is known as ***unit production***.

J103 Each application of a production rule in reverse in bottom-up parsing is known as ***reduction***.

J104 In bottom-up parsing, the RHS of a rule to which a reduction is applied is known as ***handle***.

J105 Top-Down parsing starts with the ***start symbol*** and applies the production rules by replacing ***LHS (Left-Hand Side)*** of the rule with ***RHS (Right-Hand Side)*** of the rule until the ***sentence*** is derived.

J106 Bottom-Up parsing starts with the ***sentence***, and applies the production rules by replacing ***RHS (Right-Hand Side)*** of the rule with the ***LHS (Left-Hand Side)*** until the ***start symbol*** is derived.

J107 Three commonly used techniques for capturing the meaning (describing semantics) of a program are ***Denotational***, ***Operational*** and ***Axiomatic*** semantics.

J108 Axiomatic semantics is based on ***mathematical logic***.

J109 Denotational semantics is based on ***recursive function theory***.

J110 ***Operational*** semantics is based on descriptions of state changes as the program executes.

J111 The data structure mapping each symbol in the source code to associated information such as location, type and scope is known as the *symbol table*.

J112 Type information can be stored in either the *syntax tree* or in the *symbol table*.

J113 The commonly used data structures for the symbol table are *List*, *Linked List*, *Hash Table*, and *Binary Search Tree*.

J114 LL(1) parser cannot handle a grammar that has *left recursion* or *common prefixes* (in RHS of productions).

J115 *Bottom-up* parsing starts with the sentence (input string of terminals), and arrives at the start symbol.

J116 In the parsing process of a bottom-up parser, the symbols corresponding to the *right-hand* side of a production rule are replaced with the *left-hand* side of the rule.

J117 Top-down parsing starts with the *start symbol* and ends with the *sentence of terminals*.

J118 The most common techniques for rewriting grammars to make them amenable for LL(1) parsing are *left recursion elimination* and *left factorization*.

J119 LR parsers belong to the category of *shift-reduce* parsers.

J120 LR(1) parser is also known as *Canonical LR* parser.

J121 In a CFG, a production in the form $X \rightarrow aX$ where 'a' is a string of terminals is called a *right recursive* production.

J122 In a CFG, a production in the form $X \rightarrow Xa$ where 'a' is a string of terminals is called a *left recursive* production.

J123 The top-down parsing is completed when it arrives at *the sentence of terminals*.

J124 The bottom-up parsing is completed when it arrives the *start symbol*.

J125 For lexical analysis, specifications are traditionally written using **_regular expressions_**.

J126 The **_lexical analyzer_** performs syntax analysis at the lowest level of program structure.

J127 The algorithms used in the parsers of compilers used in practice have a complexity (in terms of N, the length of string to be parsed) of **O(N)**.

J128 A bottom-up parsing starts with the **_sentence_**.

J129 A bottom-up parsing (assuming no errors) ends with the **_start symbol_**.

J130 **_Bottom-up_** parsing starts at the leaves of the parse tree, and works back to the root.

J131 Bottom-up parsing starts with the **_sentence_**, and finishes when the **_start symbol_** is reached.

J132 At every step in the reduction, the bottom-up parser replaces the **_RHS_** of a production with the **_LHS_** of that production.

J133 **_Bottom-up_** parser applies the production rules in reverse.

J134 The main decision in a **_top-down_** parser is the choice of production rule to apply.

J135 All of the leaves of a parse tree are the **_tokens_**.

J136 All of the internal (non-leaf) nodes of a parse tree are the **_nonterminals_**.

J137 **_Regular expression_** is a compact way to describe a language that can be accepted by a finite-state machine.

J138 The repeated trials of syntax analyzer to determine the correct production among multiple rules of the same production is known as **_backtracking_**.

J139 A state (an entry in the parsing table) of an SLR parsing table requesting both a shift action and a reduce action is known as **_shift-reduce_** conflict.

J140 A state (an entry in the parsing table) of an SLR parsing table requesting two or more different reduce actions is known as ***reduce-reduce*** conflict.

J141 The condition where there are several choices of production for a nonterminal during parsing is known ***conflict***.

J142 In predictive (top-down) parsing, there are only ***terminals*** to the left of the rewritten non-terminals.

J143 Replacing the part of input string that matches right-hand side (RHS) of a production with the nonterminal of the LHS of that rule is done in ***bottom-up*** parsing methods.

J144 The process of parsing is completed when the parser finishes at the start symbol starting from the input string in ***bottom-up*** parsing.

J145 In the RHS of any production of ***regular*** grammar, the terminal symbol must precede the non-terminals.

J146 ***Left factoring*** is done for a context-free grammar which fails the pairwise disjointness test.

J147 During compilation, the process of recognizing, evaluating, and reusing constant expressions is known as ***constant propagation*** or ***constant folding***.

J148 During compilation, replacing expensive operations (ex. multiplication) with equivalent but less expensive operations (ex. additions) is known as ***strength reduction***.

J149 Statements / expressions inside loops which do not change across iterations are known as ***loop-invariant code***.

J150 During compilation, moving loop-invariant code outside the body of a loop is known as ***code motion*** or ***code hoisting***.

J151 During compilation, inserting the code of function definition at the places of function calls, is known as ***inlining***.

J152 During compilation, detection of variables that are never used, and skipping operating on them, is known as ***dead store elimination***.

J153 During compilation, exchanging inner loops with outer loops in order to improve the locality of array references, is known as *__loop interchange__*.

J154 During compilation, breaking a loop into multiple loops over the same index range, with parts of the body of the original loop (to improve locality of reference), is known as *__loop fission__* or *__loop distribution__*.

J155 During compilation, eliminating loop by taking code from inside the loop and repeating it, is known as *__loop unrolling__*.

IOIOIOIOIOIOIOIOIOIOIOIOIOIOIOIOIOIOIOIOIOIOIOIOIOIOIOIOIOIOIOI

Essay-type Questions

J1 Show the Chomsky Hierarchy of language classes, and their corresponding grammars, and the automata for the recognition of the languages.

Language Class	Grammar	Automaton
3	Regular	NFA or DFA
2	Context-Free	Push-Down Automaton
1	Context-Sensitive	Linear-Bounded Automaton
0	Unrestricted (or Free)	Turing Machine

J2 Give the connections among regular grammar, regular language, regular expression, and finite automata.
Regular grammar contains the symbols and rules for generating certain strings.
Regular language is the set of all strings generated by a regular grammar.
Regular expression is a compact algebraic notation to describe a language that is generated by a regular grammar.
Finite automaton is a mechanism which recognizes/accepts a regular language (*i.e.*, one generated by regular grammar).

J3 Give the connections among context-free grammar, context-free language, BNF notation, and push-down automata.
Context-free grammar (CFG) contains symbols and rules for generating certain strings.

A Context-free language (CFL) is the set of all strings generated by a context-free grammar.

BNF (Backus–Naur Form) is a notation for representing a context-free grammar.

Pushdown automata is a mechanism which recognizes/accepts a context-free language (*i.e.*, one generated by a context-free grammar).

J4   List all the lexemes in the statement: `C = (F-32)/1.8;`

J5   What are the components of a context-free grammar (CFG)?
A context-free grammar is a 4–tuple consisting of:
1. A set of terminals
2. A set of nonterminals
3. A set of productions (rules)
4. A start symbol, which is a special non-terminal

J6   What is the format of a production in a CFG?
A production rule of a Context-Free Grammar (CFG) is of the form:
A → α, where A is any single non-terminal, and α is any combination of terminals and non-terminals.

J7   What are the main parts of a compiler?
1. Lexical analyzer (scanner)
2. Syntax analyzer (Parser)
3. Code optimizer
4. Code generator

J8   Give examples of static semantics which are not handled any CFG (Context Free Grammar).
1. Type checks during assignment
2. Checks for declaration of a variable before use.

J9   List three semantics description mechanisms.
1. Operational semantics
2. Denotational semantics
3. Axiomatic semantics

J10   When is a rule in a grammar called recursive?

When the nonterminal on the LHS of the production (rule) appears in the RHS.

J11 What is a derivation?
Derivation is the repeated applications of the productions (rules) of a grammar starting from the start symbol to arrive at the sentence (assuming no error).

J12 What is a sentential form?
Each of the strings in the steps of the derivation is a sentential form.

J13 What is leftmost (rightmost) derivation?
It is the process of expanding/rewriting/replacing the leftmost (rightmost) nonterminal in the input sentential form, with the RHS of a corresponding production rule.

J14 Consider the following grammar:
```
<assign> → <id> = <expr>
<id>     →    A | B | C
<expr>   → <id> + <expr>
          | <id> * <expr>
            | ( <expr> )
            | <id>
```

Show a parse tree and leftmost derivation for the following statements:
(a)   A = A + (B * (C + A))

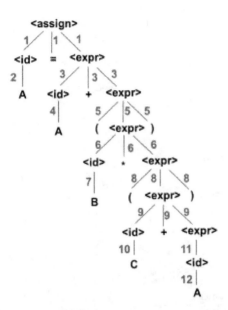

The numbers in the parse tree represent the step number in the derivation.

```
<assign>     => <id> = <expr>
        => A = <expr>
        => A = <id> + <expr>
        => A = A + <expr>
        => A = A + ( <expr> )
        => A = A + ( <id> * <expr> )
        => A = A + ( B * <expr> )
        => A = A + ( B * ( <expr> ) )
        => A = A + ( B * ( <id> + <expr> ) )
        => A = A + ( B * ( C + <expr> ) )
        => A = A + ( B * ( C + <id> ) )
        => A = A + ( B * ( C + A ) )
```

(b)   A = A * (B + C)

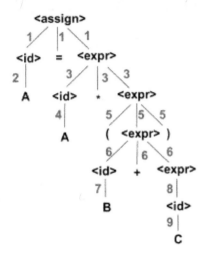

```
<assign>    => <id> = <expr>
        => A = <expr>
        => A = <id> * <expr>
        => A = A * <expr>
        => A = A * ( <expr> )
        => A = A * ( <id> + <expr> )
        => A = A * ( B + <expr> )
        => A = A * ( B + <id> )
        => A = A * ( B + C )
```

J15 Show that the following grammar is ambiguous.

```
<S>      → <A>
<A>      → <A> + <A> | <id>
<id>     → a | b | c
```

The following two distinct parse trees can be derived using leftmost derivation for the same string. Therefore, the grammar is ambiguous.

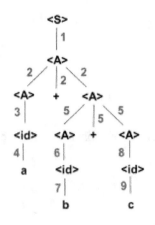 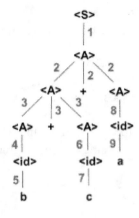

J16 Consider the following grammar:

```
S → aS | bS | a
```

Give the derivation for: **abaaba**
```
S => aS
        => abS
        => abaS
        => abaaS
        => abaabS
        => abaaba
```

J17 Consider the following grammar. Show the parse tree and leftmost derivation of the sentence "**bbaab**"

```
S → AaBb
A → Ab | b
B → aB | a
```

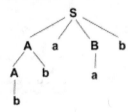

```
S => AaBb
   => AbaBb
   => bbaBb
   => bbaab
```

J18   Consider the following grammar.

```
S → AaBb
A → Ab | b
B → aB | a
```

Show the parse tree and left-most derivation for the sentence "**baaab**" using the above grammar.

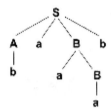

```
S => AaBb
  => baBb
  => baaBb
  => baaab
```

Show the leftmost derivation of the sentence "**bbbaaab**" using the above grammar.

```
S => AaBb
  => AbaBb
  => AbbaBb
  => bbbaBb
  => bbbaaBb
  => bbbaaab
```

J19   Consider the following production rules:
```
S → aS | bS | a | b
```

Which of the following are valid sentences generated by applying the production rules? (Show by √ or X)
1. **aaabb**   √
2. **ababab**   √
3. **aabbaa**   √
4. **baabbb**   √
5. **bbbaaba** √

J20 Consider the following production rules:
```
S → aRb
R → aR | Rb | a | b
```

Which of the following are valid sentences generated by applying the production rules? (Show by √ or X)
1. **aaaab** √
2. **aabaa** X
3. **ababb** X
4. **abbbb** √
5. **aabbbb** √
6. **baaa** X
7. **aabb** √

J21 Consider the following grammar:
```
S → aAb | bBA
A → a | aAB
B → aB | b
```

Starting from the following sentential forms, show sequence of sentential forms and the parse tree produced by bottom-up parsing going up to the start symbol of the grammar.
1. **aaAbb**
2. **bBab**

1. **aaAbb**
aaAbb => aaABb => aAb => S

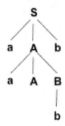

2. **bBab**
bBab => bBA => S

J22 Give the regular expression for the language generated by the following grammar.

S → aAb | aBb
A → aA | a
B → bB | b

$a^+ b^+$

J23 What is the language generated by the following grammar.

S → aSa | B
B → bB | b

$\{a^n b^m a^n, \ n > 0, \ m > 1\}$

J24 Give the regular expression for the language generated by the following grammar.

S → aRa
R → aR | Rb | a | b

$a^+ b^* a$

J25 Give regular expression for the language generated by the following grammar

S → AaBb
A → Ab | b
B → aB | a

$b^+ a^+ b$

J26 Give the regular expression for the language generated by the following production rules.

S → aS | bS | a | b

$(a \mid b)^+$

J27 Give the regular expression for the language generated by the following production rules:

S → aRb
R → aR | Rb | a | b

$(a^+ b\ b^+ \mid a\ a^+ b^+)$

J28 Write a grammar for the language consisting of the strings:
$a^n b^{2n}$, $n > 0$.

S → A
A → aAbb | abb

J29 Give the parse tree and rightmost derivation of string "**abab**" from grammar G given by S → SS | aSb | bSa | ε

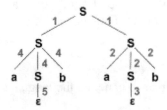

S => SS => SaSb => Sab => aSbab => abab

J30 Convert the following BNF to EBNF.

```
<stmt_list> → <stmt> | <stmt>; <stmt_list>
<stmt> → <var> = <expr>
<var> → A | B | C
<expr> → <var> + <var> | <var> - <var> |<var>
```

```
<stmt_list> → <stmt> {; <stmt>}
<stmt> → <var> = <expr>
<var> → A | B | C
<expr> → <var> [ (+ | -) <var> ]
```

J31 Describe the language generated by the following grammar:

S → A | B | a | b
A → bA | a

```
B → aB | b
```

{ab* U ba*}

J32   Give the notation and description for the language accepted by the grammar: **S → aSb | ε**.

> Notation: {$a^N b^N$ | N ≥ 0}.
> Description: Strings containing some number (≥ 0) of 'a's followed by the same number of 'b's.

J33   Give the CFG for the language {$a^n b^m$ | m > n}.

```
S → aSb | bA
A → bA | ε
```

J34   A *binary number* is any string of '0's and '1's, of length at least 1. Give the productions to generate binary numbers.

```
B → 0B | 1B | 0 | 1
```

J35   Write the productions of a grammar to generate the language:
{$a^N b a b^N$, N ≥ 0}

```
S → aSb | ba
```

J36   Show that the following grammar is ambiguous by finding a string that has two different syntax trees (**id** is treated as a terminal). Show the syntax trees.
```
A → - A
A → A - id
A → id
```

Two different parse trees are generated for the same expression. Therefore, the grammar is ambiguous.

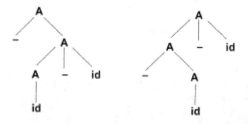

J37 Briefly describe how compilation of code into an intermediate language facilitates portability across hardware.

The file containing the intermediate code of a program in a machine *A* can be ported to another machine *B* with a different hardware (CPU). What is required on machine *B* to run the ported program is a virtual machine (an interpreter or JIT compiler) that interprets/compiles the intermediate code to the machine code of machine *B*. This is much simpler than recompiling the entire source program.

J38 What are the properties of an operator precedence grammar?

The properties of an operator precedence grammar are:
1. No production has either an empty (ε) right-hand side.
2. The right-hand side of any production does not have two adjacent non-terminals.

J40 What is the most common approach of implementing a deterministic finite-state machine (FSM)?

The most common approach of implementing a deterministic finite-state machine (FSM) is the use of a table-driven approach. Each row of the table corresponds to each state in the machine, and each column of the table for each possible character. An entry in row *j* and column *k*, Table[*j*][*k*] contains the state to go to from state *j* on character *k*.

J41 What do 'L' and 'L' denote in LL parser?

The first 'L' denotes **L**eft-to-right scanning of the input, and the second 'L' denotes use of **L**eftmost derivation.

J42 In an LL(*k*) grammar, what does the '*k*' denote?

'*k*' denotes the number of look-ahead symbols needed to choose the correct production during parsing.

J43 What do 'L' and 'R' denote in LR parser?

'L' denotes **L**eft-to-right scanning of the input, and 'R' denotes use of **R**ightmost derivation in reverse.

J44 What are the (common) LR parser variants?

SLR (Simple LR), LALR (Look Ahead LR), and CLR (Canonical LR).

J45 What do the letters in 'S', 'L', 'R' in SLR parsing denote?

'S' denotes "**S**imple", 'L' denotes **L**eft-to-right scanning of the input, and the 'R' denotes use of **R**ightmost derivation in reverse.

J46   What are non-LL(1) languages?

Non-LL(1) languages are those for which there exist unambiguous context-free grammars but no grammar for the language generates a conflict-free LL(1) table.

J47   What are the primary tasks of a lexical analyzer?

It scans the input and collects and groups characters into logical (atomic) units called lexemes and assigns them (predefined) categories called tokens.

J48   Briefly outline the three approaches to building a lexical analyzer.

1. Writing formal description (using regular grammar) of the token patterns of the language, and then using this as input to a software tool that automatically generates the lexical analyzer.
2. Designing a state transition diagram corresponding to the token patterns of the language, and writing a program which implements the state diagram.
3. Designing a state transition diagram corresponding to the token patterns of the language, and writing a table–driven implementation of the state diagram.

J48   What are the two distinct goals of syntax analysis?

1. To check the input program to determine its syntactical correctness. Upon encountering an error, it should output a diagnostic message, and recover and continue further analysis of the input program.
2. To produce a complete parse tree (or trace the structure of a complete parse tree).

J49   Why do parsing algorithms used in commercial compilers work on only a subset of all grammars?

The complexity of a general parsing algorithms for *any* unambiguous grammar is $O(N^3)$, which is not practical. By restricting the generality by considering a subset of the set of all grammars, so that the subset includes the grammar describing the programming language, the complexity of the parser can be reduced to $O(N)$.

J50   What are the two grammar characteristics that prohibit them from being used as the basis for a top–down parser?

1. Left recursion.
2. Failure of the pairwise disjointness test.

J51   Briefly describe the pairwise disjointness test.

For each non-terminal A in the grammar that has more than one right-hand side (RHS), for each pair of rules $A \rightarrow \alpha_i$ and $A \rightarrow \alpha_j$, First(α_i) $\cap$ First (α_j) = Φ

Note: First (α) = {a | α =>* aβ} (set of all terminals derived via 0 or more steps from α)

J52 What is pairwise disjointness test?

The test (check) to see if each pair of the sentential forms of multiple RHS of a production rule will not begin with the same terminal symbol (after possibly multiple derivations).

J53 Which production rule will fail the pairwise disjointness test?

A production rule with more than one RHS beginning with the same terminal (after possibly multiple derivations) will fail the pairwise disjointness test.

J54 What is a simple phrase of a sentential form?

A simple phrase (corresponding to an internal node of a parse tree) is the set of all leaves derivable from the subtree rooted at the internal node in one step.

J55 What is the handle of a sentential form?

At each step in bottom-up parsing, the specific RHS in the sentential form which is chosen to be rewritten to get the previous sentential form is called the handle.

J56 What is a recursive descent parser?

A recursive descent parser belongs to the class of top-down parsers. It consists of a set of (recursive) subprograms to process input. Each subprogram is associated with a non-terminal of the grammar and implements one of the production rules.

J57 Outline the working of LR parser.

An LR parser (Left-to-right, Rightmost derivation in reverse) reads input text from left to right (without backtracking), and produces a rightmost derivation in reverse. This is essentially a bottom-up parser.

J58 What are the advantages of LR parsers?
1. They can be built for all programming languages.
2. They can detect syntax errors as soon as possible in a left-to-right scan.
3. The LR class of grammars is a proper superset of the class parsable by LL parsers.

J59 A top-down parser builds the parse tree from the top down, starting with the start symbol. There are two types of top down Parsers:

1. Top down parsers with backtracking
2. Top down parsers without backtracking

J60 What are the main actions in top-down parsing?
1. Choose leftmost nonterminal in the current string.
2. Choose a production for the chosen nonterminal.
3. In the current string, replace the nonterminal by the right-hand-side of the rule.
4. Repeat steps 1-3 until there are no more nonterminals in the current string.

J61 What is predictive parsing?
It is a special case of recursive-descent parsing that does not require backtracking. It can determine which production to use, based on the current input symbol.

J62 What are the main actions of a Shift-Reduce parser?
1. Shift – the next input symbol is shifted onto the top of the stack
2. Reduce – The parser reduces the handle (RHS of a production) at the top of the stack to a nonterminal (the left side of the appropriate production)
3. Accept – The parser announces success
4. Error – The parser discovers a syntax error and calls a recovery routine

J63 Give the Shift-Reduce Parsing steps for the following grammar for the input string **abbcde**.

```
S → aABe
A → Abc | b
B → d
```

abbcde
⇒ **aAbcde**
⇒ **aAde**
⇒ **aABe**
⇒ **S**

J64 Outline the benefits of LR Parsing.

1. The LR parser can be constructed to recognize virtually all programming language constructs for which a CFG can be written.
2. It is the most general non-backtracking shift-reduce parsing method.
3. It handles a class of grammars that is a superset of those handled by predictive parsing.
4. It can detect syntactic errors as soon as possible with a left-to-right scan of input.
5. It can be implemented efficiently.

J65   What is a top-down parser?
A top-down parser generates parse tree for a given input using grammar productions to expand the non-terminals, by using left most derivations. It starts from the start symbol and ends with the sentence containing only terminals.

J66   What is the requirement of an operator precedence parser?
Operator precedence parser requires that two consecutive non-terminals and ε (epsilon) never appear in the right-hand side of any production.

J67   Give example of a language that context-free, but not deterministic context-free.

The language $\{x^n y^n \mid n \geq 0\} \cup \{x^n y^{2n} \mid n \geq 0\}$ is context-free. However, it is not *deterministic* context-free.

J68   Give the structure of production rules of a regular grammar.
In a regular grammar, all of the production rules are of the forms: $A \rightarrow aB$ or $A \rightarrow a$, where A and B represent single non-terminals, and a represents a terminal or the empty string.

J69   What is three address code?
Three address code (often abbreviated TAC or 3AC) is an intermediate code. It is used by optimizing compilers for making code-improving transformations. It has at most three operands and is typically an assignment and a binary operator. It is easy to generate and can be easily converted to machine code.

J70   Why is turning off the optimizer option of compiler recommended when using a source debugger?

The optimizer may change the order of the executed statements to be different from the order in the source code, which makes debugging difficult.

J71   What is the basic condition for predictive parsing?
Since there is no backtracking in a predictive parsing, it should be possible to choose a unique production based on the next input token.

J72   What is the main difference between parse tree and syntax tree?
A parse tree is an ordered, rooted tree that represents the (syntactic) structure of a sentence generated by a context-free grammar (essentially a program). A syntax tree is a tree representation of the syntactic structure of source code written in a programming language.

J73   What is left factoring?
Left factoring is rewriting a production that has right-hand side (RHS) having common prefixes, as multiple productions so that the RHS of new productions do not have common prefixes.

J74   When is left factoring used?
If there is any common prefix string for more than one production rules of a grammar, then the choice as to which of the production should be used cannot be made by the parser. In such situations left-factoring is used.

J75   Give an example of left factoring.
If A is a single non-terminal, and α, β, and γ are strings of terminals or non- terminals, then a production rule of the form:
$A \rightarrow \alpha\beta \mid \alpha\gamma$ can be left-factored into two rules of the form:
$A \rightarrow \alpha B$ and $B \rightarrow \beta \mid \gamma$, where B is a newly introduced non-terminal.

J76   Perform left factoring on the grammar production:
      A → aAB | aAc | aBc

The left factor requires creation of new production rules as follows.
              A → aA'
              A' → AD | Bc
              D → B | c

J77 List some of the limitations of syntax analyzer that are handled by the semantic analyzer.

The limitations of syntax analyzer handled by semantic analyzer are:
1. The validity of the token cannot be determined.
2. The declaration of the token before its use cannot be determined.
3. The initialization of the token before its use cannot be determined.
4. The validity of the operations performed on the token type cannot be determined.

J78 Briefly describe the difference between grammar and parser of a programming language.

A grammar of a programming language basically consists of a set of symbols (terminals and non-terminals), and a set of rules (productions) for generating the valid sentences (programs) of the language. The parser of a programming language is mechanism for recognizing the valid sentences of the language. During the process of recognition, it builds a structure which is used in the further stages of language translation to machine code.

J79 Give an outline of the operation of a bottom-up parser.
1. Start with the sentence to be parsed (initial sentential form).
2. Repeat the following steps until the start symbol is reached:
   i. Scan through the input until the RHS of one of the production rules (this is called a handle) is found.
   ii. Apply a production rule in reverse – replace the RHS of the rule which appears in the sentential form with the LHS of the rule. This is known as a reduction.

IOIOIOIOIOIOIOIOIOIOIOIOIOIOIOIOIOIOIOIOIOIOIOIOIOIOI

Books on Programming Languages and Compilers

- Robert W. Sebesta. *Concepts of Programming Languages* (12th Edition). Pearson, 2019.

- Franklyn Turbak and David Gifford (with Mark A. Sheldon). *Design Concepts in Programming Languages*. MIT Press, 2008.

- Terrence W. Pratt, Marvin V. Zelkowitz. *Programming Languages: Design and Implementation* (4th Edition). Pearson, 2000.

- John C. Mitchell and Krzysztof Apt. *Concepts in programming languages*. Cambridge University Press, 2002.

- Ravi Sethi. *Programming Languages: Concepts and Constructs* (2nd Edition). Addison-Wesley, 1996.

- Alfred V. Aho, Monica S. Lam, Ravi Sethi, Jeffrey D. Ullman. *Compilers: Principles, Techniques, and Tools* (2nd Edition). Pearson, 2007.

- Charles N. Fischer, Ron K. Cytron, Richard J. LeBlanc, Jr. *Crafting a Compiler*. Pearson, 2010.

Other Related Quiz Books

This is a quick assessment book / quiz book. It has a vast collection of over 1,100 questions, with answers on Data Structures. Questions have a wide range of difficulty levels and are designed to test a thorough understanding of the topical material. The coverage includes elementary and advanced data structures – Arrays (single/multidimensional); Linked lists (singly–linked, doubly–linked, circular); Stacks; Queues; Heaps; Hash tables; Binary trees; Binary search trees; Balanced trees (AVL trees, Red–Black trees, B–trees/B+ trees); Graphs.

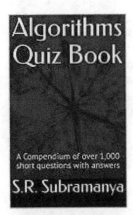

This is a quick assessment book / quiz book. It has a vast collection of over 1,000 questions, with answers on Algorithms. The book covers questions on standard (classical) algorithm design techniques; sorting and searching; graph traversals; minimum spanning trees; shortest path problems; maximum flow problems; elementary concepts in P and NP Classes. It also covers a few specialized areas – string processing; polynomial operations; numerical & matrix computations; computational geometry & computer graphics

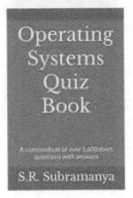

This is a quick assessment book / quiz book. It has a wide variety of over 1,600 questions, with answers on Operating Systems. The questions have a wide range of difficulty levels and are designed to test a thorough understanding of the topical material. The book covers questions on the operating systems structures, fundamentals of processes and threads, CPU scheduling, process synchronization, deadlocks, memory management, I/O subsystem, and mass storage (disk) structures.

This is a quick assessment book / quiz book. It has a wide variety of over 1,700 questions, with answers on Computer Security. The questions have a wide range of difficulty levels and are designed to test a thorough understanding of the topical material. The book covers all the major topics in a typical first course in Computer Security – Cryptography, Authentication and Key Management, Software and Operating Systems Security, Malware, Attacks, Network Security, and Web Security.

This is a quick assessment book / quiz book. It has a vast collection of over 1,200 short questions, with answers and programs, on Java programming language. The topical coverage includes data types, control structures, arrays, classes, objects, and methods, inheritance and polymorphism, exception handling, and stream and text I/O

This is a quick assessment book / quiz book. It has a vast collection of over 1,200 short questions, with answers and programs, on C++ programming language. The topical coverage includes data types, control structures, arrays, pointers and reference, classes and objects, inheritance and polymorphism, exception handling, and stream and text I/O.

This is a quick assessment book / quiz book. It has a vast collection of over 1,100 short questions, with answers and programs, on C programming language. It covers all the major topics of C programming – data types, operators, expressions, control structures, pointers, arrays, structures, unions, enumerated types, functions, dynamic storage management, I/O and Library functions.

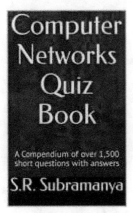

This is a quick assessment book / quiz book. It has a vast collection of over 1,500 short questions, with answers. It covers all the major topics in a typical first course in Computer Networks. The coverage includes, the various layers of the Internet (TCP/IP) protocol stack (going from the actual transmission of signals to the applications that users use) – physical layer, data link layer, network layer, transport layer, and application layer, network security, and Web security.

www.ingramcontent.com/pod-product-compliance
Lightning Source LLC
LaVergne TN
LVHW051445050326
832903LV00030BD/3251